Risk Disclosure

Futures and Forex trading contains substantial risk and is not for every investor. An investor could potentially lose all or more than their initial investment. Risk capital is money that can be lost without jeopardizing one's financial security or lifestyle. Only risk capital should be used for trading and only those with sufficient risk capital should consider trading. Past performance is not necessarily indicative of future results.

Hypothetical Performance Disclosure

Hypothetical performance results have many inherent limitations, some of which are described below. No representation is being made that any account will or is likely to achieve profits or losses similar to those shown; in fact, there are frequently sharp differences between hypothetical performance results and the actual results subsequently achieved by any particular trading program. One of the limitations of hypothetical performance results is that they are generally prepared with the benefit of hindsight. In addition, hypothetical trading does not involve financial risk, and no hypothetical trading record can completely account for the impact of financial risk of actual trading. For example, the ability to withstand losses or to adhere to a particular trading program in spite of trading losses is a material point that can also adversely affect actual trading results. There are numerous other factors related to the markets in general or to the implementation of any specific trading program that cannot be fully accounted for in the preparation of hypothetical performance results and all of which can adversely affect trading results. This book is for educational purposes only and the opinions expressed are those of the author only. All trades presented should be considered hypothetical. None of the trades are traded in a live account.

Testimonials

Testimonials appearing in this publication may not be representative of other clients or customers and are not a guarantee of future performance or success.

Contents

My Story

Hello, my name is Dale, and I've been a full-time trader since 2008. I have always been very passionate about economics, finance, and trading. I got my university degree in finance before becoming a certified portfolio manager and an investment manager, as well as getting my financial derivatives certification. Unlike most of the other trading "gurus," I am proud to say that I have a proper education and trading certifications. Of course, this is thanks to my parents, who supported me enormously in my studies and at the start of my career.

Fresh out of college, I started to work as a market analyst for a major brokerage. Most would be grateful to have this position right out of college, but I didn't really feel that way. I had two problems with this job. The first one was that I didn't like having a boss who told me what to do. I always studied hard to be independent, not an employee. The second reason was that I didn't particularly appreciate how the company treated its customers. I think this is an issue with most Forex brokers. They don't really care if their clients make money or not. They are selfish and focus primarily on their fees. They feel no responsibility, and they don't care about their clients' best interests. I didn't like being a tool in such a company, so I left.

After I quit my job, I focused all my efforts on trading. I started by testing numerous trading strategies, trying different trading approaches, backtesting various patterns, and anything else you can think of for 12–15 hours every day.

I was trading various instruments and using many different trading styles. I was trading stocks, investment certificates, and automated trading systems. Currently, my primary focus is on manual currency trading.

When I started trading currencies, I was under the impression that I needed to find a Holy Grail, which would make me a big pile of money quickly. I was searching for this Holy Grail among various trading indicators. I tried most of the standard indicators with many different settings, but nothing worked, at least not in the long run.

My first tangible success was when I finally got rid of all the indicators and started anew with simple Price Action. For the first time, I felt I was getting somewhere! The big "eureka moment" came when I combined Price Action with Volume Profile.

At first, I was trading only swing trades. I was working mostly on a daily time frame and, as you can imagine, I did not have many trades. Still, this was the first time I felt confident about my trading. I was also thrilled that I had finally found my way and that my trading had become consistent.

For many people this would be enough, but I wanted to learn more and go further. I started to go much deeper, and I began to look for a method or a tool suitable for day trading on much faster time frames.

Why I Started Using Order Flow

At first, I was using Price Action and Volume Profile, but I wanted more, so I went into tape reading using DOM (Depth of Market). DOM is a feature that shows all the orders that appear in the market—including the "pending orders."

DOM (Depth of Market):

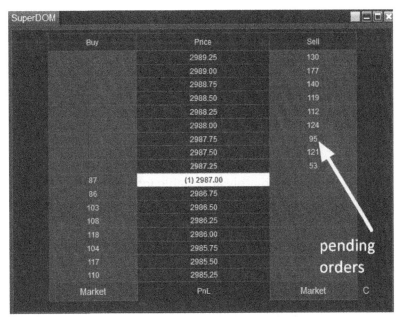

This seemed like the right way to go until I realized that most pending orders never get filled. These orders are only placed in the market to move the price in the desired direction. When the price comes close to them, they are, in most cases, withdrawn. Sort of like a carrot in front of a donkey, he remains in constant pursuit but never actually gets it.

For me, DOM was just full of noise and too hard to read. I knew there was a lot of useful info there, but I needed something to help me read that crazy matrix. This is where the Order Flow came into play.

The big advantage of using the Order Flow is that it prints orders that matter—orders that actually got filled (not the pending orders, which are often never filled). Order Flow also prints those orders in a way that is much easier to read as well as backtest. Exactly the thing I needed!

At first, I started to use a third-party Order Flow software. After some time, I came up with a few ideas for how the Order Flow could be improved by adding some specific and helpful features. Long story short—I had a custom-made Order Flow developed with the additional features built in!

Now I use my Order Flow every day for my intraday trading. I prefer to use it with Price Action and Volume Profile as those show me the bigger picture. Still, there are others who prefer to use Order Flow as a standalone indicator you build your trading around.

What Will You Learn?

This book aims to give you precise, immediately actionable info without wasting your time on unnecessary filler and fluff. It's the type of book I would love to have had when I started to learn how to trade with the Order Flow. Here is what you can look forward to learning:

- Choosing the right trading platform for Order Flow trading
- NinjaTrader 8 platform – introduction
- Choosing the right Order Flow software
- Where to get data for Order Flow
- The best instruments to trade with Order Flow
- Order Flow – what it tells us
- Order Flow – special features
- How to set up Order Flow workspace
- Order Flow – trading setups
- Order Flow – confirmation setups
- How to use Order Flow to determine your Take Profit and Stop Loss
- How to use Order Flow for trade management
- How to find strong institutional Supports and Resistances using Volume Profile
- How to combine Order Flow with Volume Profile

All that in a straightforward way with many pictures and examples.

E-book Download

A quick note before we begin: If you purchased a printed black-and-white version of this book, then I expect you will find some details in pictures a bit challenging to see and some text or numbers too small and difficult to read.

For this reason, I uploaded an electronic version of the book (along with some Order Flow videos) on a special webpage. This way, you will be able to check the pictures in color and high resolution. If needed, you can also zoom in to see the images better.

Link: https://www.trader-dale.com/of-book/

Password: happy trading

Important Notice

Before we jump straight into it, I need to tell you that this is not a magic "get rich quick" guide. The Order Flow is a fantastic tool, and the strategies I am going to show you are the best-proven strategies I know. BUT this alone won't make you a great trader. Just like getting a new Ferrari does not make you a better driver. You need to practice and you need hands-on experience. You must spend time and energy learning to trade with the Order Flow yourself! Hands-on experience cannot be learned from a book!

So, if you don't mind that I won't be giving you a "magic pill" (as it doesn't exist), let's move on to the first chapter!

Setting up Order Flow

NinjaTrader 8 Trading Platform

The trading platform I use for running Order Flow is NinjaTrader 8. I have been using NinjaTrader 8 for many years, and I highly recommend it.

A significant advantage of NinjaTrader 8 is that it is a free platform. Yes, really. It has a free mode, which is without any restrictions and has all its functions enabled. I have never had a reason to switch to their paid version, which shows how cool the free version is.

Also, all the indicators I have developed for NinjaTrader 8 platform (Volume Profile, VWAP, and Order Flow) work with the free version.

The way I do it is that I do my analysis on the NinjaTrader 8 platform, but when it comes to trade execution, I do it on another platform with my broker.

There is a shortlist of brokers that you can connect to NinjaTrader 8 and trade straight from this platform, but, in my opinion, there are better and cheaper brokers around than those who are supported by NinjaTrader 8. For this reason, I use the NT8 only for charting, and I execute the trades elsewhere. This may seem like a disadvantage, but I believe that being able to choose your own broker is worth it.

Here are some useful links for you:

NinjaTrader 8 platform download: https://ninjatrader.com

My preferred broker: https://www.trader-dale.com/forex-brokers

Other Trading Platforms

A persistent question I get is whether Order Flow can run on the Metatrader 4 platform. While it may be possible, there are too many limitations and problems. MT4 is a 15+-year-old software, and trying to run Order Flow there would be like placing an engine from a Ferrari into an old, half-broken budget car thinking you would start winning races with it.

A lot of people also like using TradingView for their charting. It is a fine platform, but, unfortunately, you can't run Order Flow there.

There are also some other charting platforms; one of the most famous (apart from NinjaTrader) is Sierra. This platform is not free, though; you need to pay monthly fees to use it.

Data Feed for Order Flow

Order Flow shows all executed Buy and Sell orders traded in the exchange. To see those orders, you need an excellent data feed that gives you Bid and Ask data. Such data is often referred to as "Level 1" data.

There is also "Level 2" data, but you won't need that. Level 2 data includes market depth, which the Order Flow does not use (that is only useful, for example, when tape reading).

Since Order Flow is best used with centralized markets, I suggest you use it with Futures data. My recommended data provider is CQG.

CQG – Futures Data Feed

You can get a free trial data feed connection here: https://ninjatrader.com/FreeLiveData

This trial CQG connection will expire after some time, and then you will have two options. The first option will be to create a new trial using a different email address. The second option will be to start paying monthly fees for the data feed.

I don't think there is a better way to get free Futures data anywhere without limitations.

If you need a connection for any specific trading instrument, then the best way is to email NinjaTrader support directly and tell them what you need. They will help with any questions and give you a quote for that particular data feed connection.

They usually respond quickly, and they are very helpful overall. You can contact them via email here: platformsupport@ninjatrader.com

Where to Get Order Flow

If you search the internet, you will discover many Order Flow software options available. The price ranges from around $100 to $5,000, with some costing even more!

Let's first talk about the cheap ones. As with many things in this world, here also applies: *"You buy cheap, you get cheap."* If you manage to purchase Order Flow for $100 somewhere on the internet, don't expect the functionality to be any good. You also can't expect any help or service from the software provider either.

The other extreme is Order Flow software for thousands of dollars. In my experience, those are full of many tweaks and features a real trader does not really need. They are there only to justify the high price. Also, in my experience, such software is often developed by coders who are not real traders. They don't know what an Order Flow trader really needs. Those guys usually code any feature they can think of (useful or not), and they add it to their software. This way, their Order Flow looks full of cool features to justify the higher price.

The ideal solution is to get your Order Flow software from a real trader who developed it by working hand in hand with the software developer.

When I was working on my Order Flow software, I made sure of two things: First, the core of the Order Flow was 100% working, was well optimized, and worked with various trading instruments. Second, the unique features my Order Flow had were all useful and helpful in real trading. My software has no redundant features or added black-box indicators, of which nobody really knows what they do or how they are calculated. I am really proud of the special features we built into the software, and I cannot wait to show you later in this book!

If you decide to get my custom-made Order Flow software (along with further Order Flow training), you can get it here:

https://www.trader-dale.com/order-flow-indicator-and-video-course/

What Instruments Can You Trade with Order Flow?

Order Flow is best used for day trading. The most popular markets are:

- Currency Futures / Forex
- Indices Futures (S&P 500, Nasdaq, Dow Jones, DAX...)
- Oil, Metals (Gold...)
- Stocks

I use Order Flow mostly for currency Futures. As I mentioned before, I do my analysis on NinjaTrader 8 using currency Futures. I then execute the trades with my Forex broker in the spot Forex market.

Which Trading Instrument Should You Start With?

I recommend starting with just one trading instrument, for example 6E (EUR Futures), and focusing solely on that. The reason is that every trading instrument behaves differently. Every instrument or market has a different average volume traded, different times when it is most active, different reactions, etc. It takes a lot of time just to master one instrument!

Professional day traders often focus only on one trading instrument they have mastered and which they trade. When starting, I don't see an advantage to choosing many markets as it will just complicate the learning process.

I focus primarily on the 6E (EUR Futures). This is where I feel most comfortable and where I have by far my best trading results.

Order Flow: Forex vs. Futures

"Why do we need to use Futures instead of Forex?" That's a good question I get quite often. The distinction between these two is this:

Futures: Is centralized, which means that everybody on the planet sees the same price and volumes traded. Most importantly, Futures allow us to see how much volume was traded on the Bid as well as the Ask.

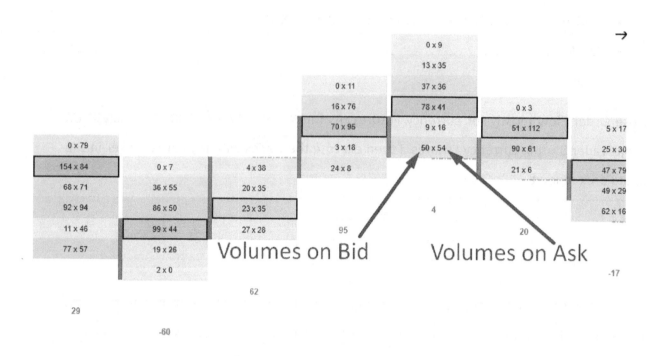

Forex: Is decentralized, which means that only people who use the same data feed provider see the same price and volumes. Data from each data provider can differ a bit. Not too much, but the difference is there. The main disadvantage to Futures is that Forex providers are unable to distinguish Bid and Ask (or if they do, they do it very badly). So, the best you can get is Total volume (= sum of Bid + Ask).

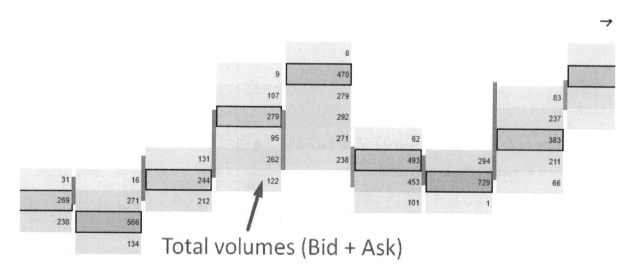

Transferring Trading Levels from Currency Futures to Forex

Because I do my analysis on currency Futures but then execute my trades in the Forex market, I need to transfer my Support/Resistance levels from Futures to Forex.

Transferring levels from EUR and AUD Futures to EUR/USD and AUD/USD (Forex) is pretty simple. You place the two charts next to each other, visually compare, and then transfer the level from left to right. It is pretty simple to find the level because the correlation is virtually 100 % (the charts look the same).

Transferring levels gets more challenging with the CAD, JPY, and CHF Futures because the correlation is -100 %, which means the charts are inverse. Also, one pip on Futures doesn't equal one pip on Forex. With CAD, JPY, and CHF futures, I still transfer the levels "visually," but you need to imagine the Forex chart is reversed. It takes some time and effort to do this a few times a day, but with some practice, you will be able to do it quickly. It's very similar to learning to ride a bike; once your brain gets it, it gets it!

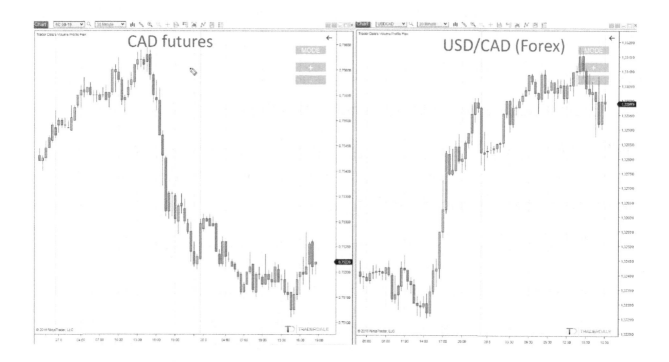

Order Flow – Market Participants

Most people get confused when they open an Order Flow chart for the very first time. There is no shame in that. Order Flow shows so much information that it is easy to get overwhelmed if you don't know what to look for! Don't worry though; by the time you have finished this book, you will be able to read Order Flow without getting a headache :)

Let's start by going through the basic stuff, like what Order Flow shows and how to read it.

Passive vs. Active (Aggressive) Market Participants

To learn what is going on in the Order Flow chart, you first need to understand one fundamental thing: the distinction between passive and active market participants. This may sound like too much theory, but this piece of information is vital. If you are not sure you got it the first time, go through it again. If you don't get this point now, you will be lost later. Ready? Here we go!

Passive Market Participants

Passive market participants are traders who enter their trade with a limit (pending) order.

They do not chase the market. They wait for the price to come to them and then they enter their trades only for the price they want (or better).

Every subject in the market can be a passive participant. It does not matter if it is a bank, a pension fund, a hedge fund, or a private trader like you or me. It is merely everybody who enters a trade with a limit order. If you place a limit order in your trading platform, you are a passive market participant.

When the price hits the limit order you placed in the market, the order gets filled, and you get into the trade (you have just opened a trading position). This trading position will show on the Order Flow footprint.

If you open a LONG position with a limit order, then it will appear on the BID side of the footprint (on the left).

If you opened a SHORT position with a limit order, then it will appear on the ASK side of the footprint (on the right).

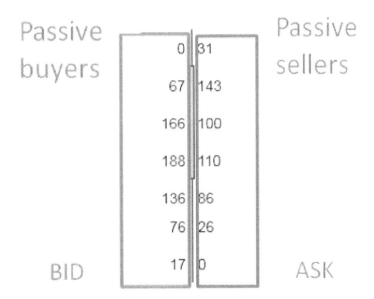

So far, so good? This will make things a bit more complicated:

Active Market Participants

Active market participants are traders who enter their trades with market orders. If you press a market Buy or Sell, then you are an active market participant. Your position will get filled immediately.

No matter where the price currently is, no matter where exactly the trade is going to be filled, aggressive participants just want in. Now! Even if this means risking a slippage (the trade won't open precisely at the price where they pressed the Buy/Sell).

A market order is useful in situations where there is no time to wait to get your whole position filled exactly at the price you wanted. For example, this could be when there is a quick price movement that you don't want to miss.

If you open a LONG position with a market order, it will appear on the ASK side of the footprint (on the right).
If you open a SHORT position with a market order, it will appear on the BID side of the footprint (on the left).

Active and Passive in One Chart

The distinction between passive and aggressive market participants is what makes so many people confused. It is the main reason they cannot use Order Flow properly and struggle to make money with it, which is why I stress the importance of this point!

Let me give you two more pictures that sum this up. If you are not 100% confident with where the passive and aggressive traders show on the footprint, then I suggest you print those pictures where you can see them while trading.

The picture below shows two identical footprints and the two ways you can interpret them.

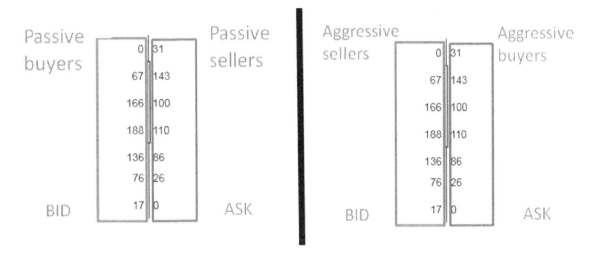

Let me put all that into one footprint that sums this all up:

What the picture above says is this:

- **BID:** Shows <u>aggressive Sellers</u> and <u>passive Buyers</u>.
- **ASK** (Offer): Shows <u>aggressive Buyers</u> and <u>passive Sellers</u>.

If you understood this, then your first question will probably be, *"How am I supposed to know if the number that just appeared on the ASK is from a passive Seller or an aggressive Buyer?"*

I am afraid you will not like the answer as there is no way to know with absolute certainty!

The good news is, in this book, I am going to teach you how to make a reasonable estimate, which will allow you to make the correct assumption in most cases. Not in all cases—I do not teach magic as I warned you already.

Bigger Perspective (BONUS)

To put things into a bigger perspective, let me show you one more thing. Maybe you have seen some Volume Profile indicators with two colors and the developers told you that one color shows Sellers and the other color shows Buyers. Like this one, for example:

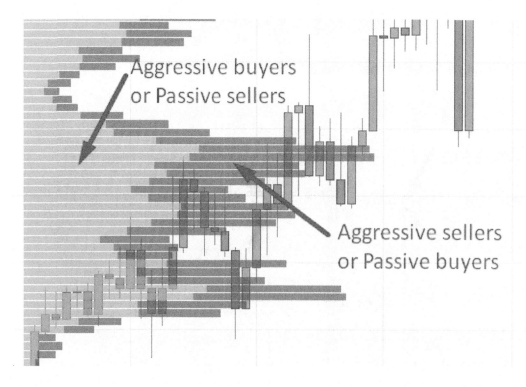

If somebody tells you such a thing, then they clearly don't know what they are talking about.

Based on what I just taught you, you now know that when volumes appear on BID, they can be both aggressive Sellers or passive Buyers. And when volumes appear on the ASK, they can be both aggressive Buyers or passive Sellers! If somebody tells you that "green" means Buyers and "red" means Sellers, they are telling you a half-truth.

Order Flow – Basic Chart Description

In this chapter, I am going to describe standard Order Flow software and describe its primary interface. You can apply this to most of the common Order Flow software as the core should be the same for each of them.

Footprints

The Order Flow does not show standard candles, but it shows FOOTPRINTS.

A footprint shows not only Open, High, Low, Close as standard candles do, but it also shows orders that got traded within that candle.

Orders are placed on Bid or on Ask. When a BUYER enters a Long trade (with a market order), then his position shows on the ASK side of the footprint. When a SELLER enters a Short trade (with a market order), his position shows on BID.

This is how the Order Flow chart is drawn:

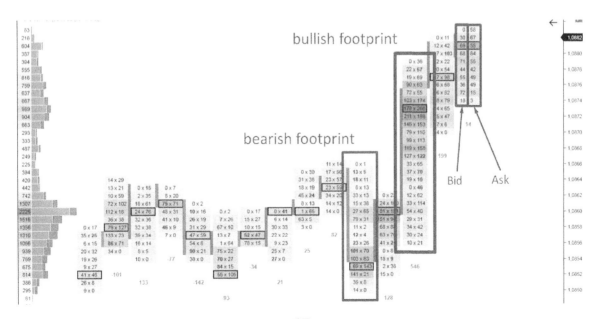

Green/Red Cells

Inside every footprint there are green or red cells.

The cell is GREEN if the number on the Ask is larger than the number on the Bid.

It is RED when the Bid is larger than the Ask.

Simply put, this represents the strength of Buyers versus Sellers.

However, as you learned in the previous chapter, this is not always true, and there is much more to it. But for the sake of keeping this part simple, let's leave it at that and revisit it when we talk about Order Flow strategies.

Usually (not always), the bullish footprints are primarily green (stronger Buyers) and the bearish footprints are primarily red (stronger Sellers).

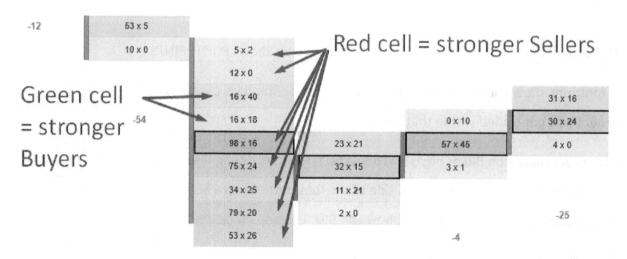

High Volume Nodes (HVN)

Possibly, the most important place in any footprint is the High Volume Node. It represents the place where the heaviest volumes were traded, a place where the institutions were the most active. It is marked by a black outline, making it easily visible at first sight.

If there are more Heavy Volume Nodes at the same price, in two or more consecutive footprints, then my proprietary Order Flow software will make it in yellow. Price levels like these represent Support/Resistance zones.

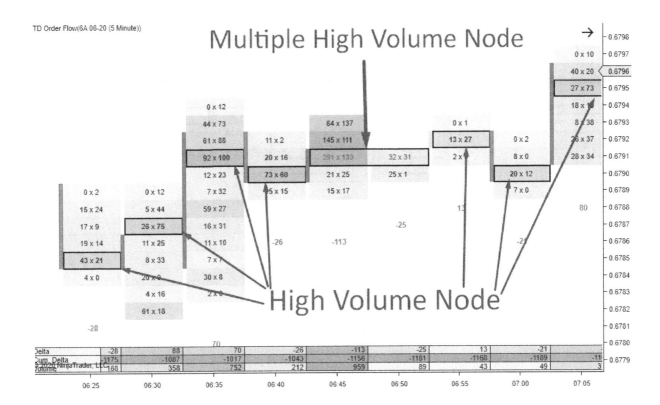

Delta

Below each footprint (the place could vary depending on the software you use) there is a number that is either green or red.

It is GREEN (positive) when more volume is executed at the Ask (in that whole footprint).

It is RED (negative) when more volume is executed at the Bid (in that whole footprint).

This essentially tells you who is stronger in that footprint—Buyers or Sellers. Bullish footprints have a positive Delta (GREEN). Bearish footprints typically have a negative delta (RED). This holds true primarily in trending markets.

If there is a rotation, then you cannot rely on this as much. The reason is that in a rotation, big institutions usually enter their trades both with market and pending orders. They combine these two types of orders in an effort to mask their true intentions.

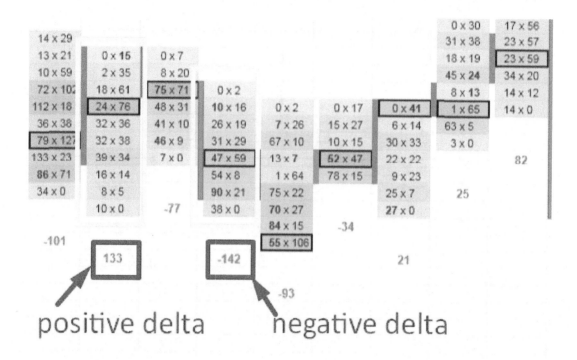

What should grab your attention is when you see a bullish footprint with a negative Delta or a bearish footprint with a positive Delta.

A bullish footprint with a negative Delta tells you this: The price is rising, but Sellers are entering their Shorts and they are stronger than the Buyers.

A bearish footprint with a positive Delta tells you this: The price is falling, but Buyers are entering their Longs and they are stronger than the sellers.

Both those scenarios represent a warning that a price reversal might happen (price reverses to follow Delta).

EXAMPLE: Price and Delta Divergence

Let me give you an example of a trade I had a couple of days ago on EUR Futures:

1. I had identified a strong level of Resistance on the EUR/USD using Volume Profile. I published this Resistance level a week ago publicly on my website.
2. I waited almost a week until the price reached this Resistance.

3. When it did, there was a strong uptrend the whole day. It would be risky to enter a Short trade from Resistance against this strong uptrend. For this reason, I used my Order Flow software to identify precisely when Sellers started showing up around this Resistance.

4. In the Order Flow, I looked at 6E 12-20 instrument, which is EUR futures. It 100% correlates with EUR/USD (Forex), where I place my trades. The reason I looked at Futures was that I needed to see the separate Bid x Ask volumes and Delta (which Forex does not show).

5. When the price reached the volume-based Resistance, there was a significant divergence between price and Delta. Price was rising, but Delta was falling! This meant that even though the price was going up, strong and aggressive Sellers were jumping in more and more! This is one of my favorite trade confirmations, so I jumped in the Short trade.

6. I took a 10 pip Take Profit quite easily. I didn't want to try to take more out of this because the EUR was in a strong uptrend. Trading Shorts against a strong uptrend is risky, so it was better to take a smaller profit and quit the trade.

This is what I saw when I entered the short trade (price rising, Delta negative).

* BTW. This picture shows footprints with Total Volumes (sum of Bid + Ask).

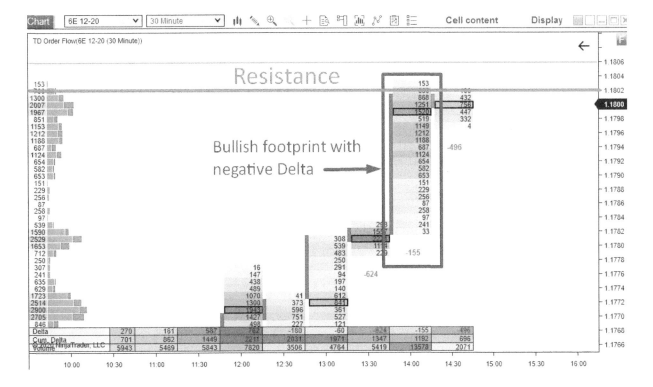

This was the reaction:

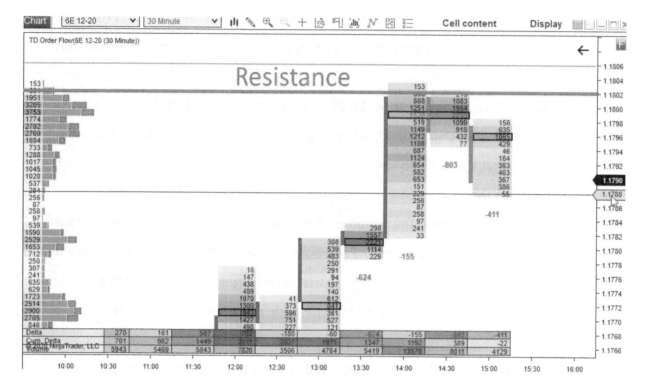

There was a bit more to this trade, which I will not mention here for the sake of simplicity. What I want you to focus on is the divergence between rising prices and falling Delta. That was what predicted the turning of the price.

If you would like to see the whole trade and how it went in real-time, then you can watch the video where I recorded it all. It is on my website, and you can access it using the link and password I gave you at the beginning of this book. Enjoy!

Footprint Summary

The panel at the bottom of the Order Flow chart shows a summary of each footprint.

You can set it in any way you want to show only the information you need for your strategy. It is best not to have too much summary info there and solely focus on the most important things.

Here is a picture that shows the whole summary panel:

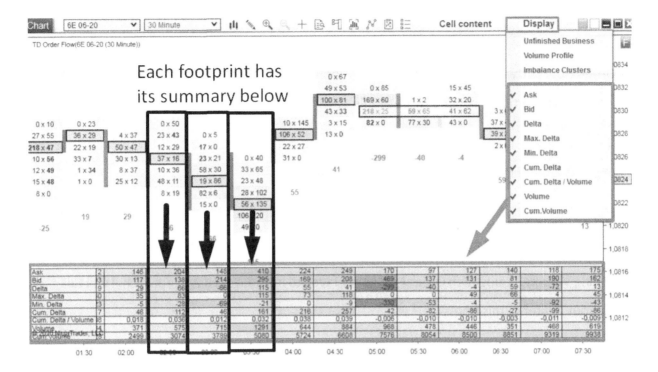

Such a panel is quite standard for much Order Flow software. Developers like to boast of how many useful things it shows. The truth is you won't need all those features as they distract from the more critical aspects. I personally only use Delta, Cumulative Delta, and Volume. It gives me this quick overview info:

Delta: Shows whether there were stronger Buyers or Sellers.

Cumulative Delta: Shows Delta changes throughout the whole day.

Volume: Shows the accumulative volume of each footprint.

The screenshot below shows my summary settings:

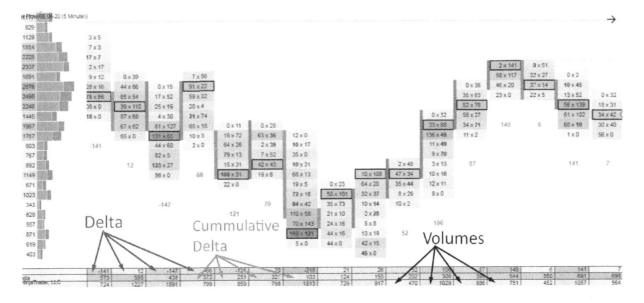

Volume Profile

My Order Flow software has its own Volume Profile. It is a Daily Volume Profile that shows the volume distribution throughout the whole day.

This is a significant feature because it shows you the bigger picture, which is critical when trading with Order Flow!

The BLUEISH/GREEN color on the Volume Profile represents orders traded on the Ask, and the RED color represents orders traded on the Bid.

Combining Volume Profile with Order Flow is my favorite intraday trading approach. I will talk more about it later in this book.

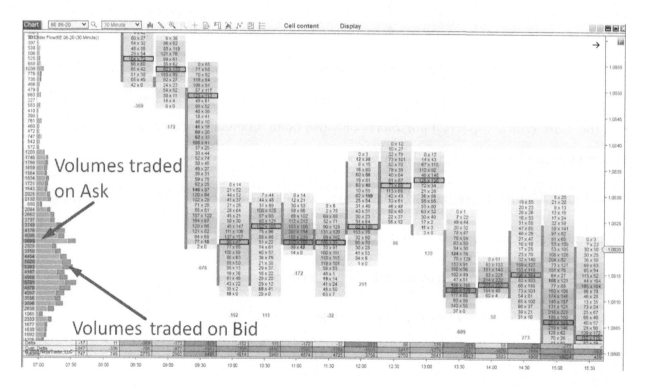

TD Order Flow – Special Features

Here I will continue describing more useful Order Flow features. But this time, the features won't be standard; instead, they are unique to my Order Flow software.

Order Flow for Forex

One of my Order Flow software's most unique features is that you can use it for trading Forex. This is not very common because Order Flow is primarily used with centralized data (Futures).

Still, NinjaTrader has a good Forex data feed with reliable volume information. We were able to use this and adjust the Order Flow to work even with Forex!

The Forex data they prove does not give Bid and Ask volume, only Total Volume (= sum of Bid and Ask). For this reason, you cannot use all the Order Flow functions when trading Forex (functions using Bid and Ask). Still, the Volume data is extremely useful, and the Order Flow gives you a tremendous edge even without separate Bid and Ask volume.

Order Flow used with Forex Volume data looks like this:

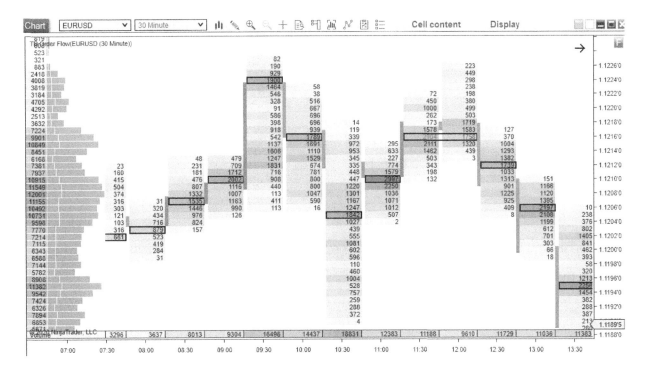

Every cell shows volumes that were traded at the given price level; the heavier the volume at a given price point the darker the shade.

Volume Clusters

When trading with the Order Flow, it is very important to pay attention to heavy volume areas as well as low volume areas. This would be almost impossible if you just looked at the numbers in each cell without having any visual help.

For this reason, I designed my software to recognize heavy volumes and use darker colors to make the heavy volume areas stand out. This way, you can immediately identify heavy volume areas at a glance.

When there is an area that is way darker than the surrounding areas, it marks a place where the BIG trading institutions and their algorithms were most likely actively trading.

Those are critical areas to keep track of as they often represent strong Support and Resistance zones.

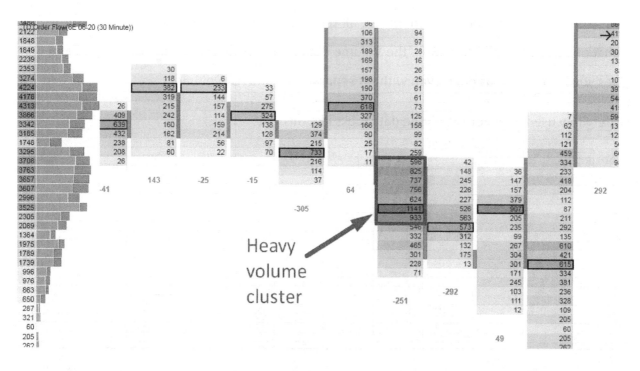

Those darker and lighter shades are also used on the Bid x Ask visualization as you can see in the chart that follows.

The heavier the volumes the darker the color:

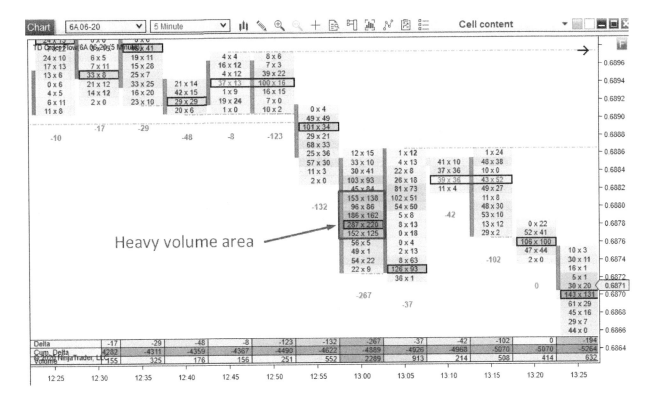

Multiple High Volume Nodes (HVN)

A very important place in every footprint is the High Volume Node. It is the place where most of the volumes got traded (Bid and Ask combined).

An extremely strong level is formed when two or more High Volume Nodes meet at the same price in consecutive footprints. When two nodes meet, I call it a Double Node, when it is three nodes, then a Triple Node, etc...

My software automatically detects those Multiple HVNs and highlights them in yellow. This way, you can quickly identify them at first sight.

Those Multiple HVNs are very significant in my Order Flow analysis because they often represent strong Support and Resistance zones.

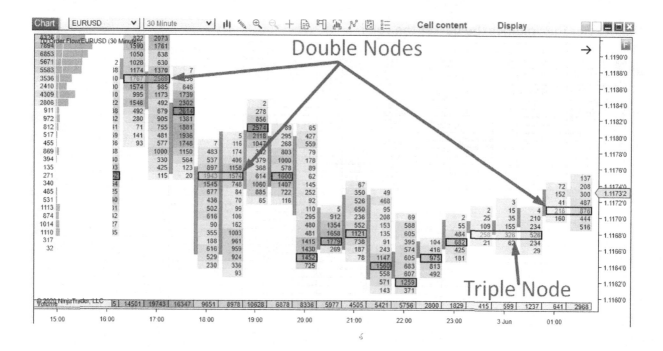

Imbalances

Imbalances are a great way of tracking market sentiment. Only with Order Flow will you be able to see this type of market detail!

An Imbalance is when Buyers are way more aggressive than Sellers or when Sellers are more aggressive than Buyers.

If Buyers are way more aggressive than Sellers (Ask is 300% or larger than the Bid), then the number on the Ask is printed in BLUE.

If Sellers are more aggressive than Buyers (Bid is 300% or larger than the Ask), then the number on the Bid is printed in BLUE.

Bid x Ask Order Flow is compared diagonally, which means that Imbalances are compared as shown below (this is also how you read the Order Flow footprint—diagonally):

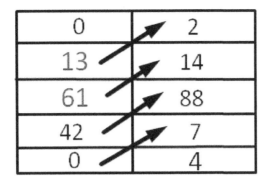

The picture above shows two Imbalances. One Imbalance is in the second row and the other one is in the third. The reason is: 13 is 300% or more than 2, and 61 is 300% or more than 14.

You will often see Imbalances at the start of a strong and aggressive trend and within the trend itself.

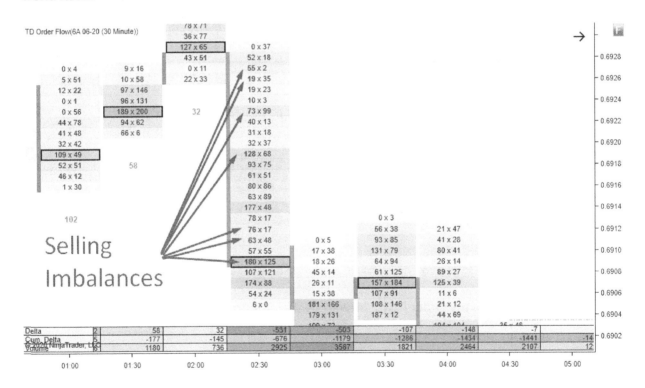

Stacked Imbalances

Stacked Imbalances are three or more cells with imbalances on top of each other. Learning to spot these areas is extremely important to us traders because they often represent strong Support and Resistance zones.

Stacked Imbalances are a sign that one side of the market (Buyers or Sellers) is dominating and in control. Those Buyers or Sellers are really strong, aggressive, and determined to push the price their way.

My Order Flow software automatically highlights areas with Stacked Imbalances. Those areas represent strong Support and Resistance zones.

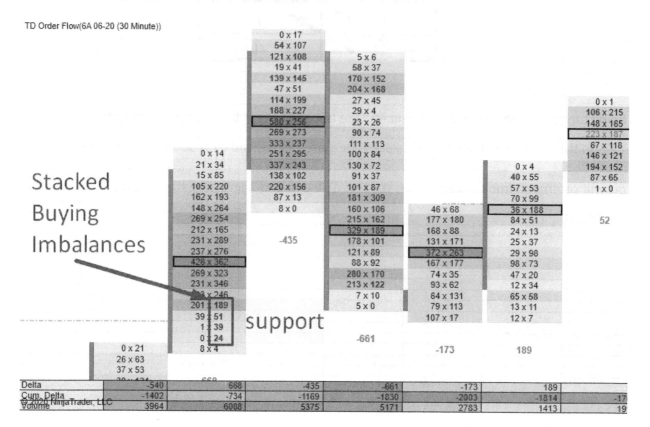

Delta	-540	668	-435	-661	-173	189	
Cum. Delta	-1402	-734	-1169	-1830	-2003	-1814	-17
Volume	3964	6088	5375	5171	2783	1413	19

Unfinished Business

Another unique feature of my Order Flow software is that it automatically detects Unfinished Businesses (Failed Auctions).

Unfinished Business represents a market imperfection. It shows that the high or low, which was just formed, was not formed properly.

What do I mean by "formed properly"?

Every footprint represents an auction process. This process needs to end in a certain way. A properly formed high needs to have 0 contracts traded at the Bid, and a properly formed Low needs to have 0 contracts traded on the Ask.

When the market turns from a new low or high without this happening, it is called Unfinished Business (or a Failed Auction).

It is an imperfection that the market tends to fix. The price has a tendency to revisit such places and "finish the business." You can think of these areas as a sort of magnet to the price.

My Order Flow automatically detects these areas and draws a line there. This line is left in place until the price revisits it and fixes this market imperfection.

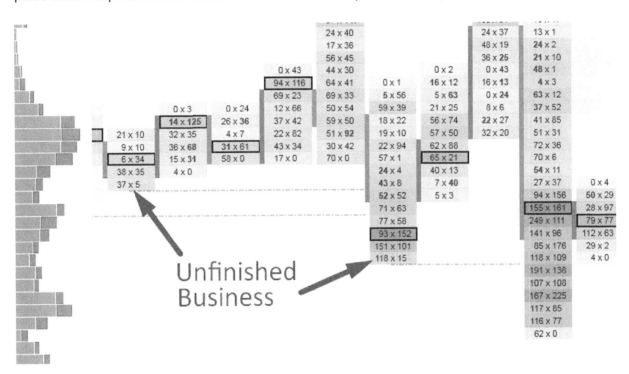

Let me give you a live trading example from one of my recent trades on EUR Futures.

EXAMPLE: Unfinished Business

I was in a Short trade, and I was deciding whether to take a 10 pip profit or take a half profit at both 10 and 20 pips. Because there was Unfinished Business where the chart had previously turned, I decided to take just the 10 pip profit. It would have been risky to try to go for more because the Unfinished Business could work like a magnet and drive the price upwards (against my Short).

Here is a screenshot from the live session video:

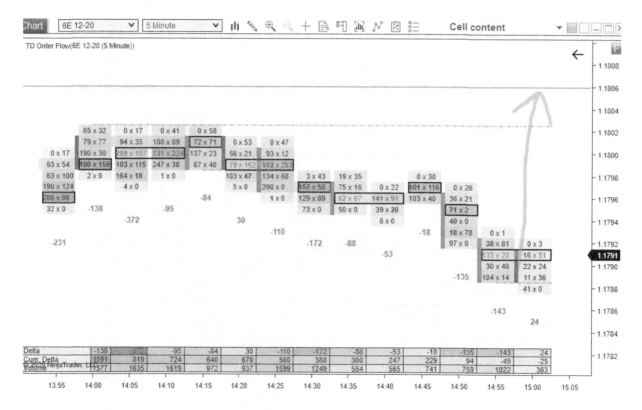

The picture shows the Unfinished Business (the green dotted line) and a red arrow, which I drew to demonstrate what could happen there.

Later, the Unfinished Business did end up working as a magnet, and the price went upwards to test it as shown here:

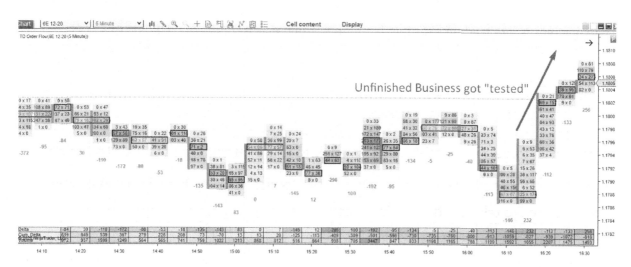

This allowed me to quit the trade with a profit before the price would have turned against me.

The first thing many people think when they hear about Unfinished Business is that this is the Holy Grail. Unfortunately, it does not work like that. The reason is that the price could move quite a significant distance away from the Unfinished Business without actually testing it.

In my trading, I don't rely on the Unfinished Business indicator too much. Instead of a Holy Grail, I consider it a small helper when making trading decisions as in the trade illustrated above.

Trades Filter

This unique feature filters out all the noise from the market and leaves only the biggest trades (trades of the BIG guys we want to track).

It makes the Order Flow easy to read, and you can be sure you won't miss any significant market action! When the BIG guys are present, it will show on the Trades Filter.

You can set the Filter anyway you like—depending on how much "noise" you want to filter out. I personally prefer to set it in a way that only the most significant trading orders show. This means that on EUR Futures (my favorite day trading instrument) I have the Trades Filter set to 25. This means it only shows executed trades that were 25+ contracts.

You may say that 25 contracts are not that much and you are right. But you need to consider this: Institutions prefer to enter their trading positions using Iceberg orders. This means that they open positions with multiple orders rather than with one single order like a retail trader.

But when there is not much time, and the institutions need to get into their trade quickly, they don't have the luxury of Iceberg orders and they need to enter their trades using bigger position sizes. Those larger orders are the ones we track with the Trades Filter.

Later in this book, I will show you an excellent trading strategy based solely on the Trades Filter.

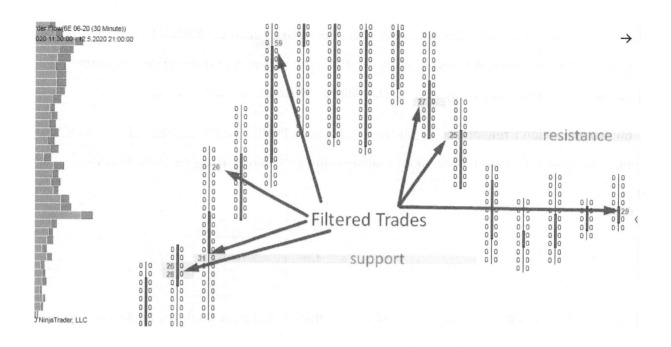

Cumulative Delta

This is a separate indicator, which is usually not a part of Order Flow software. But it works so nicely with the Order Flow that it would be a shame not to use these two together! For this reason, I decided to add this standalone indicator to my Order Flow software so you can use them together.

The Cumulative Delta prints the difference between the Bid and Ask. You can think of it this way (even though it is not 100% correct, as you have already learned): Cumulative Delta identifies the difference between Buyers and Sellers.

If there are more aggressive Buyers jumping in, then the Cumulative Delta is rising. If there are more aggressive Sellers than Buyers, then it is falling.

It is best to watch the Cumulative Delta around strong Support and Resistance zones. If strong Buyers or Sellers start to enter their trading positions there, then Delta will show you!

What I really like is to look for divergences between price and Delta on the 1 Minute chart.

EXAMPLE: Cumulative Delta

The price is heading downwards, but the Cumulative Delta is going up. This tells me that even though the price is going down, there are Buyers entering Long and the price will most likely reverse and turn upwards.

It is best to look for price x Delta divergences around Support and Resistance zones.

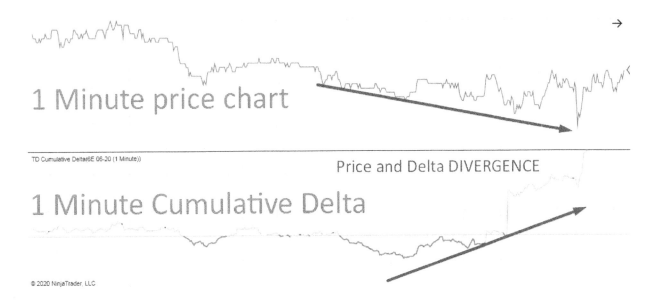

1 Minute price chart

TD Cumulative Delta(6E 06-20 (1 Minute))

Price and Delta DIVERGENCE

1 Minute Cumulative Delta

Order Flow – Trading Workspace

Since you now know what the Order Flow shows and you are familiar with its major features, let me show you what my trading workspace looks like. You can set yours up exactly the same way as I have it. If you shoot me an email (contact@trader-dale.com) I can also send you my workspaces so you don't need to set them up yourself.

Let me now show you what my Order Flow screen looks like:

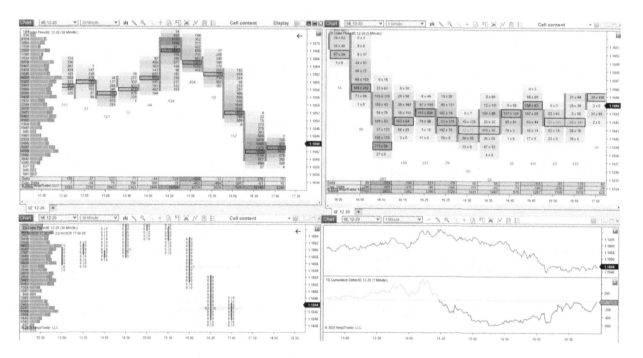

My Order Flow screen shows four charts. Those charts are linked together so they always show the same trading instrument.

Top left chart: This one shows the bigger picture. It shows the 30 Minute footprint. The cells in each footprint show "total cell volume" (Bid + Ask). Below each footprint (the green or red number) is the footprint's Delta.

On the left side, there is the Daily Volume Profile. In the summary below, I have Delta, Cumulative Delta, and Volume.

Top right chart: This one is a more detailed chart for spotting the orders as they are filled in the market. I use it for trade entries and exits. It is a 5 Minute chart, which shows the Bid and

Ask in each cell. Each footprint also has Delta printed below. The trade summary at the bottom shows Delta, Cumulative Delta, and Volume.

Bottom left chart: 30 Minute Order Flow chart with Trades Filter and Daily Volume Profile on the left. I use this chart to filter out the noise and to look for the big trading orders.

Bottom right chart: Shows 1 Minute price chart at the top and 1 Minute Cumulative Delta chart at the bottom.

This workspace allows me to see all the important things that are going on in the market.

I can see the big picture with the 30 Minute Volume chart and Trades Filter as well as the more granular details on the 5 Minute Bid x Ask chart and on the Cumulative Delta chart.

Order Flow – Trading Setups

In this section, I am going to show you five of my favorite Order Flow trading setups. You can trade these as standalone setups, which means that they are strong just on their own. There is no need to combine them with any other setup, nor do you need to look for any additional trading confirmation (you can do that, but it is not a must). Let's get to it then!

Trading Setup #1: Volume Clusters

This setup is based on trading significant areas of heavy volume (Volume Clusters), which occurred either in a <u>trend</u> or in a strong <u>rejection</u> of higher/lower prices.

Such heavy volume areas are places where the BIG guys (institutions) and their trading algorithms placed a large portion of their orders.

Let's first talk about the situation when the Volume Cluster occurred within a trend.

*This strategy does not use Bid x Ask, only the Volume setting. Because of this, you can trade it also on Forex (still, I recommend doing your analysis on Futures).

Volume Clusters (within a TREND)

The exact steps to follow are:

1. Set your Order Flow software to show Volumes (not Bid x Ask). This will make it way easier to identify heavy volume zones. This way, the Order Flow will show shades of grey and the heavy volume areas will stand out more.

2. Find a trend and look for dark grey areas (heavy Volume Clusters) that stand out. Those areas represent heavy volumes (institutional activity).

3. You need to see the price move away from the Volume Cluster, making at least one or two whole footprints (candles) above or below the heavy volume area. I like to use the 30 Minute footprint chart for this.

4. Then you need to wait for a pullback. When the price returns back to this heavy volume area, you enter your trade.

5. Your trade entry should be at the beginning of the Volume Cluster or at the place where the volumes were the heaviest (within that Volume Cluster).

6. If the heavy volume area was formed in an uptrend, then you go Long. If it was formed in a downtrend, you would look to go Short.

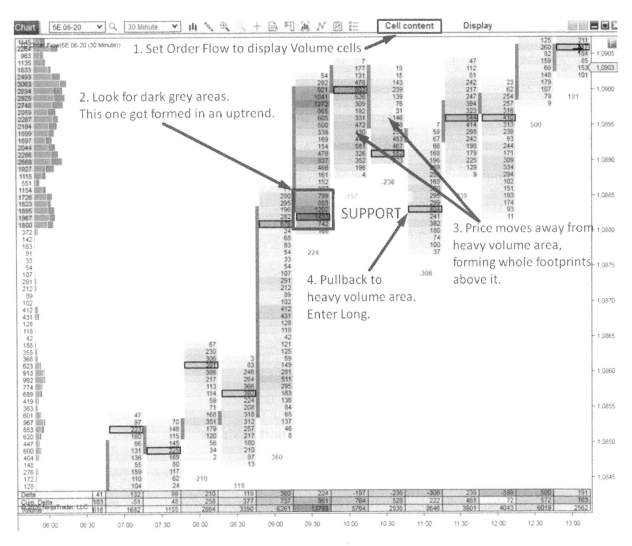

LOGIC BEHIND THIS

Let me describe the logic behind this setup with the picture above. First, there was an uptrend, and Buyers were pushing the price upwards. Then they started to add massively to their Long positions (around 1.0880). We can see this place nicely with the Order Flow—that's the Volume Cluster. From this place, the price continued to move upwards. The Buyers were still dominating the market and they were pushing the price up. When the price made it back into this Volume Cluster again, those Buyers wanted to defend their

Long position, which they entered in the Volume Cluster. As a result, the Buyers began aggressively buying again (with Market Orders) to push the price away from this critical level.

Another aspect that helped drive the price upwards from the Volume Cluster was Sellers closing out their Short trades. When the price made the pullback to the Volume Cluster, it was the Sellers who drove it there. Likely, those Sellers knew about the strong Volume Cluster around 1.0880. They knew that strong Buyers were adding to their Longs massively there and that it was an important level for them. So, instead of risking a fight with strong Buyers, the Sellers quit their Short trades as the price reached the Volume Cluster. It's important to understand that when Sellers close their Short trades, they need to close them with a Long order. In this case, this added to the Longs of the aggressive Buyers who were defending the Volume Cluster.

TWO FACTORS

In the end, two factors drove the price upwards from the 1.0880 Volume Cluster:

#1 factor: Buyers defending their Long Position

#2 factor: Sellers quitting or closing out their Short Position

We can't really tell which of these factors played a bigger role (because both Buyers and Sellers used Buy Market Orders—the same orders). The important thing is that both these factors were pushing the price the same way—upwards.

This kind of logic is also used in my other Order Flow trading setups. It does not apply only to the Volume Cluster setup.

Let me follow with a couple of examples of the Volume Cluster setup:

Example #1: Volume Cluster (within a trend)

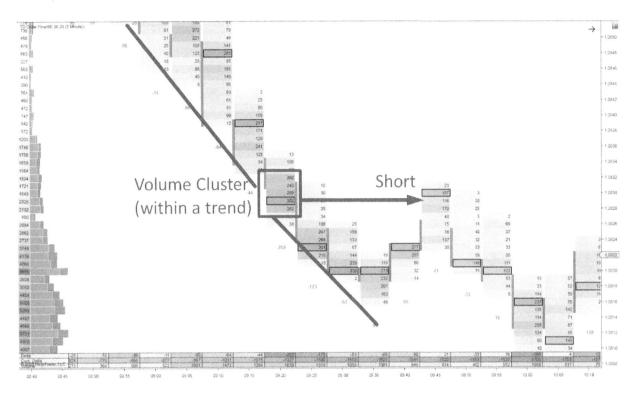

Example #2: Volume Cluster (within a trend)

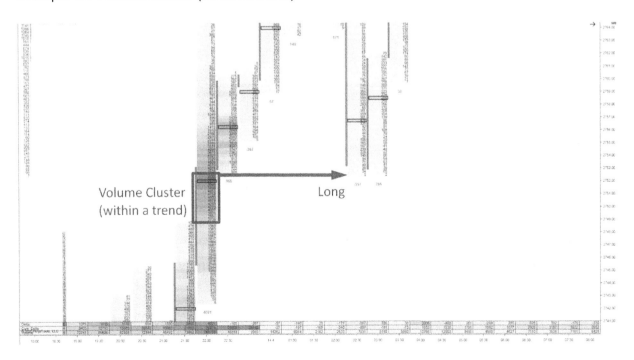

Example #3: Volume Cluster (within a trend)

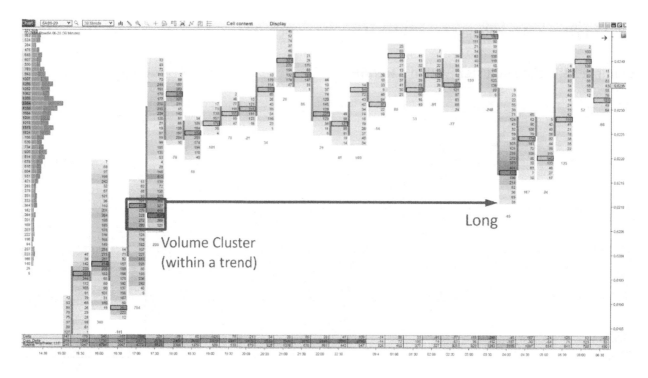

Volume Cluster
(within a trend)

Long

Example #4: Volume Cluster (within a trend)

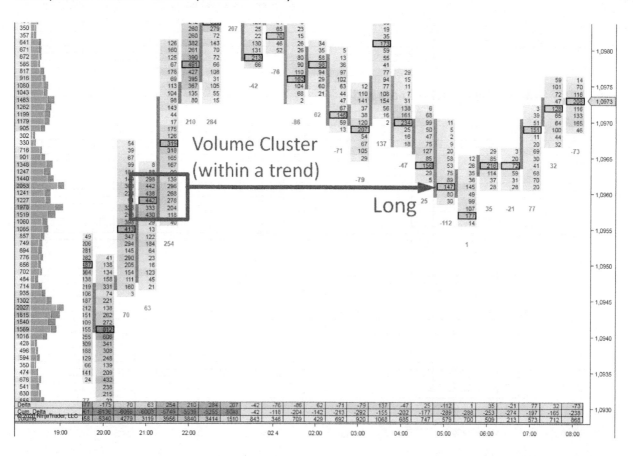

Volume Cluster
(within a trend)

Long

Volume Cluster (within a REJECTION)

This is very similar to the previous trading setup. The only difference is that (in step 2) you look for the significant Volume Cluster in a strong rejection of lower or higher prices (not in a trend).

A strong rejection of higher prices is when the price goes aggressively upwards and then it suddenly turns and goes into a rapid sell-off (= higher prices got rejected). A rejection of lower prices is the same, only reversed.

The picture below shows a strong rejection of higher prices:

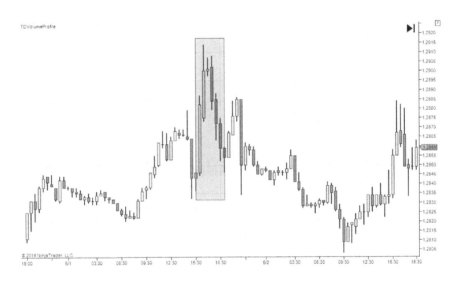

Here is the complete guide step by step:

1. Set your Order Flow software to show Volumes (not Bid x Ask). This will make it way easier to identify heavy volume zones. This way, the Order Flow will show in shades of grey and the heavy volume areas will stand out more.

2. Find a strong rejection of higher or lower prices and look for dark grey areas (Volume Clusters) that stand out. Those show heavy volumes (institutional activity).

3. You need to see the price move away from the Volume Cluster making at least one or two whole footprints (candles) above or below this area. I like to use the 30 Minute footprint chart for this.

4. Then you need to wait for a pullback. When the price returns back to the Volume Cluster, you enter your trade.

5. If the Volume Cluster got formed in a rejection of lower prices, you look to go Long (in the direction of the rejection). If there was a rejection of higher prices, you look to take a Short trade.

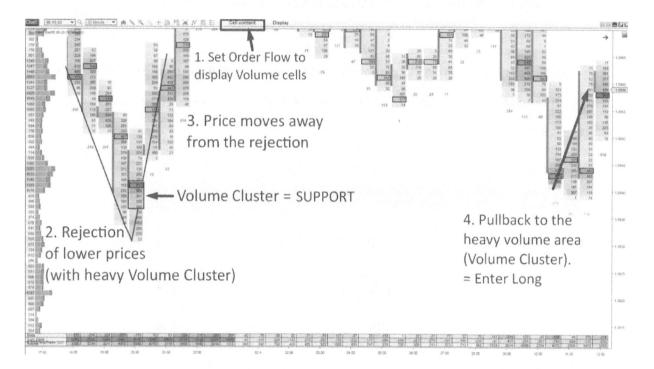

The logic behind this setup is the same as with the Volume Clusters in a trend mentioned earlier. In this case, the strong Buyers entered much of their position in the Volume Cluster created during the initial rejection. As the price later retested this area, those Buyers were defending their Longs and Sellers abandoned their Shorts.

Example #1: Volume Cluster (within a rejection)

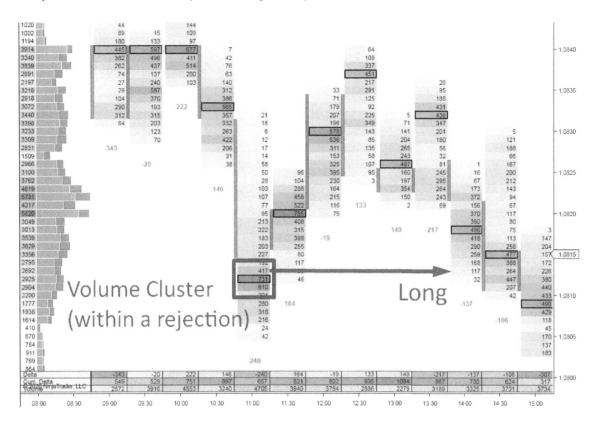

Example #2: Volume Cluster (within a rejection)

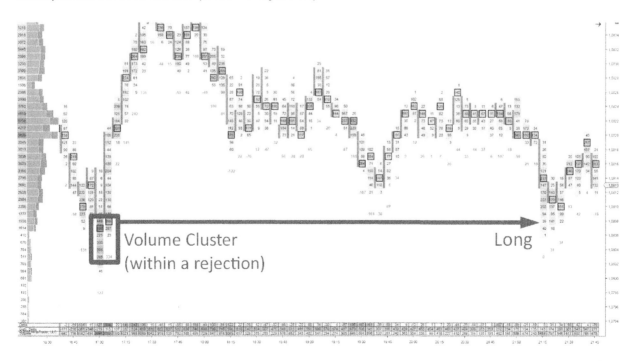

Example #3: Volume Cluster (within a rejection)

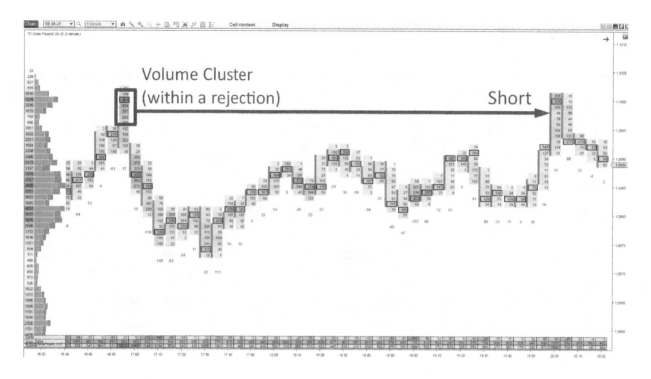

Example #4: Volume Cluster (within a rejection)

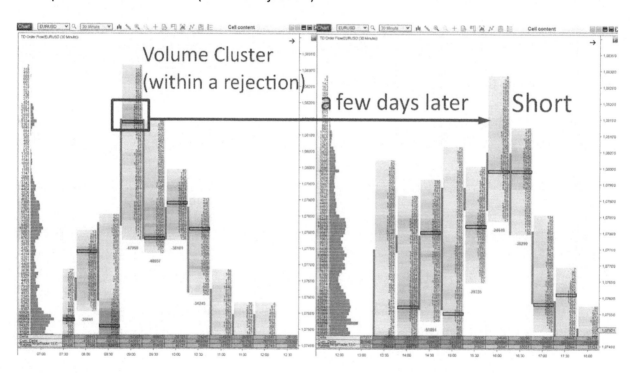

Trading Setup #2: Multiple Nodes

This setup is designed to track institutional trading activity using the High Volume Nodes (HVN). The HVN shows where the heaviest volumes were traded within one footprint by creating a black outline around that cell.

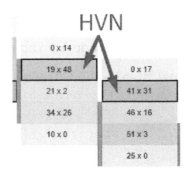

This setup focuses on finding two consecutive footprints that have their HVNs at the same price level—this is what I call the "Multiple Node." This tells us that in both these footprints the most important price level was the same. Therefore, we can assume that this level is important.

In this setup, the minimum number of footprints with HVNs next to each other is two. If there are more, then the level is even stronger.

I look for the Multiple Nodes in these significant areas:

- Within a trend
- Before a trend
- In a strong rejection of higher/lower prices

This trading setup does not use Bid x Ask, so you can apply it to spot Forex as well (I still recommend Futures though).

The concrete steps to trading the Multiple Nodes setup are:

1. Set your Order Flow so it shows Volumes (this is only my preference. You can also use Bid x Ask setting). My preferred time frame is the 30 Minute chart.

2. Identify a place where there are more HVNs next to each other (= Multiple Node). This place needs to form before the start of the trend, within a trend, or in a strong rejection of higher/lower prices.

3. There need to be at least two whole footprints formed AFTER the Multiple Node was formed. Those footprints need to be completely above or below the Multiple Node.

4. Wait for a pullback to the Multiple Node.

5. Enter a trade. If the price hits the Multiple Node from above, then go Long. If the price hits the Multiple Node from below, then go Short. Trade only the first touch (first test).

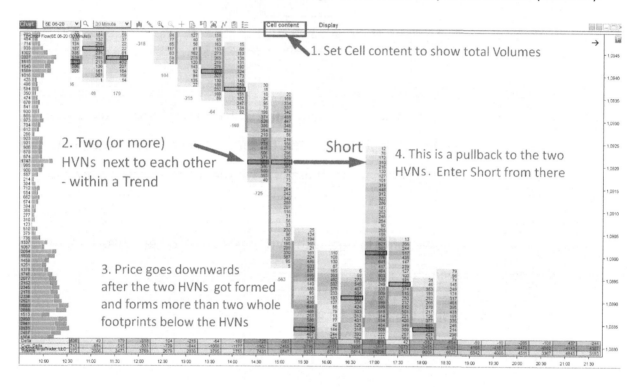

EXAMPLES: Multiple Nodes

Example #1: Multiple Nodes (in a Trend)

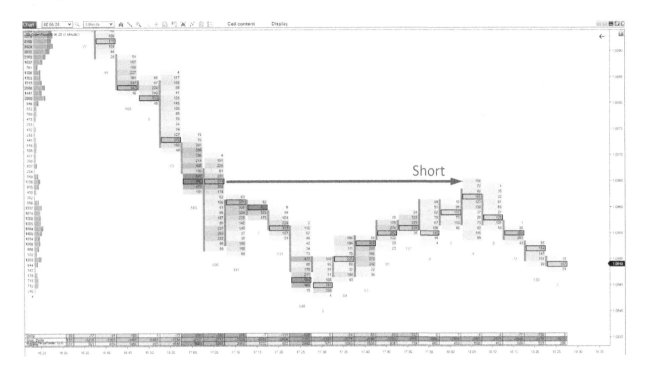

Example #2: Multiple Nodes (in a Trend)

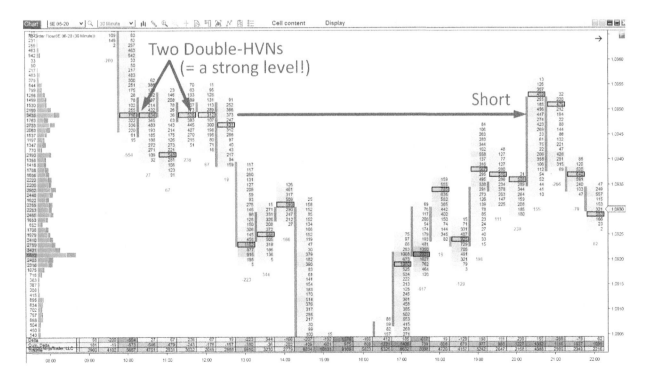

Example #3: Multiple Nodes (before a Trend)

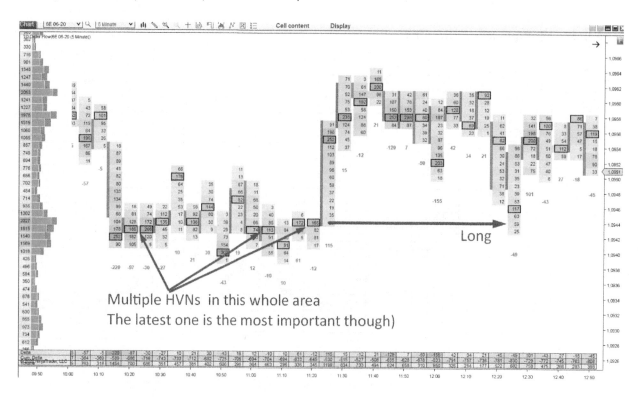

Multiple HVNs in this whole area
The latest one is the most important though)

Example #4: Multiple Nodes (before a Trend)

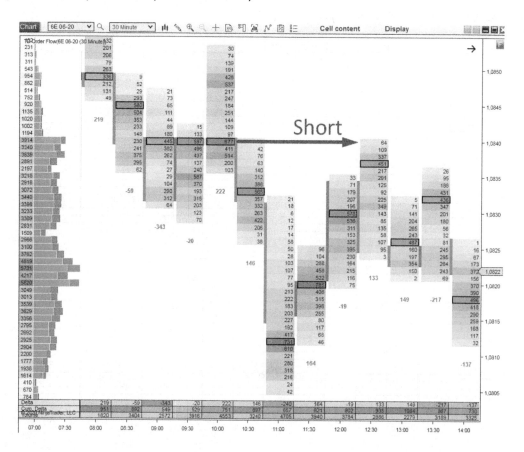

Example #5: Multiple Nodes (in a strong rejection of higher/lower prices)

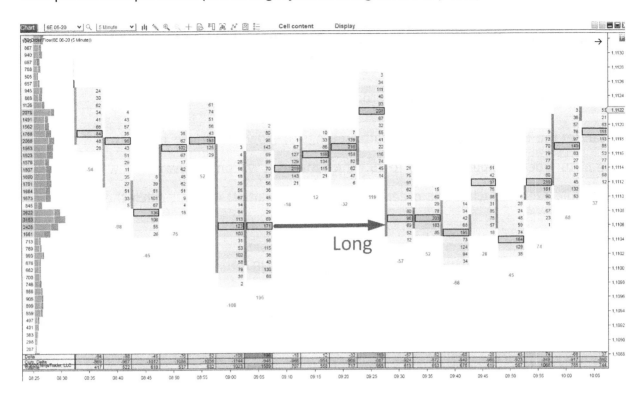

Example #6: Multiple Nodes (in a strong rejection of higher/lower prices)

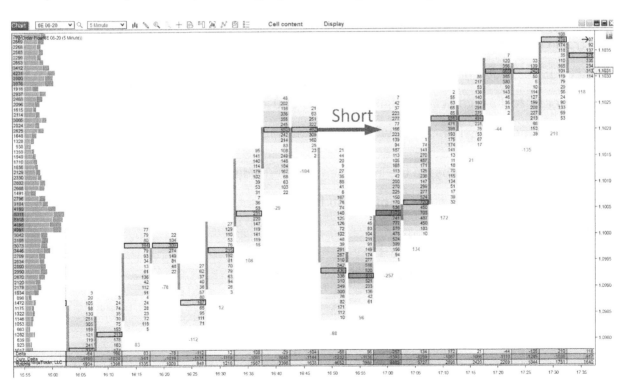

Trading setup #3: Trades Filter

The Trades Filter setting is a unique feature of my Order Flow software. It enables you to filter out the market's noise and display only the largest trading orders (the BIG guys). This simple strategy is based on following those big orders.

You can set the Trades Filter in the indicator settings to show only trades bigger than X lots. In the picture below, I put the filter to 25, which means it will only show trades with more than 25 lots executed with ONE order (as I mentioned earlier, it won't catch the Iceberg orders).

I currently use this setting with currency Futures (mainly EUR futures – 6E):

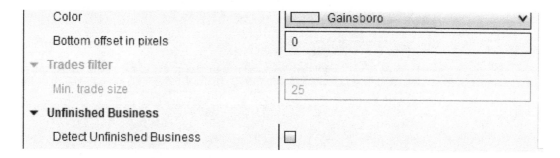

Every trading instrument has its own specifics and different volumes. The 25 lot setting suits currency Futures, but it does not work, for example, on the ES (S&P 500 futures). There the number needs to be significantly higher—around 300 or more. Also, heavy volumes are traded only in the US session, so you won't get any signals during the EU or Asian session.

You need to adjust this number to the instrument you're trading and, in some cases, the time of day you're trading as well. A rule of thumb here is to set it to a number that gives you around 5–10 trading signals per day.

Let's now talk about the setup so all this becomes clearer.

The setup is very similar to Setup #1: Volume Clusters. Here are the steps:

1. Set your Order Flow to show Bid x Ask. Then enable the Trades Filter in the Indicator settings and set the minimum trade size (for EUR Futures, I use 25 lots).

2. Look for highlighted values (red/green) on the Trades Filter—values that are not 0. Those are big trading orders that work as strong Support and Resistance zones.

3. You need to see the price move away from such an area first, making at least one or two whole footprints (candles) above or below this area. I like to use the 30 Minute footprint for this.

4. Then you need to wait for a pullback. When the price returns to this big order area, you enter your trade.

5. If the price hits this area from above, then you enter Long. If it makes a pullback from below, then you go Short. Green does not mean you go Long and red does not mean you go Short!

6. Trade only the first hit (first test). Don't attempt to trade one trading level more than once, as the probability of a 2nd successful reaction to the same level is smaller.

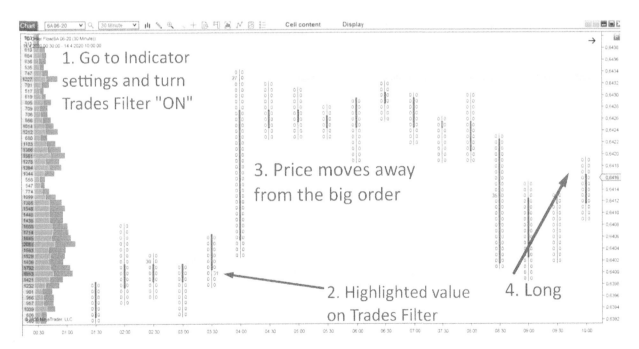

You can trade this setup as a standalone setup, or you can decide to trade it after you see the entry point gets confirmed by any of the "trade confirmation" setups taught in this book.

*BTW – If you decide to use my Order Flow software, you will also receive my trading workspaces. This way, you actually won't need to set the Trades Filter yourself.

EXAMPLES: Trades Filter

Example #1: Trades Filter

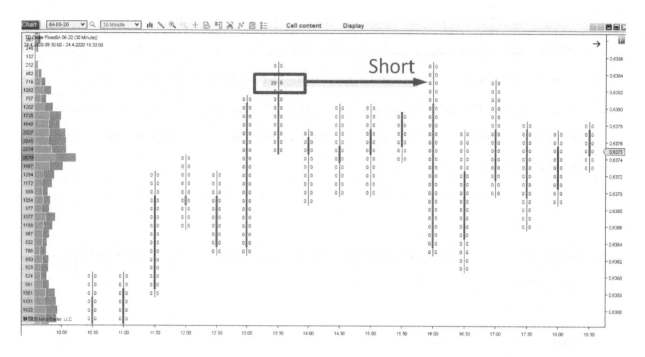

Example #2: Trades Filter

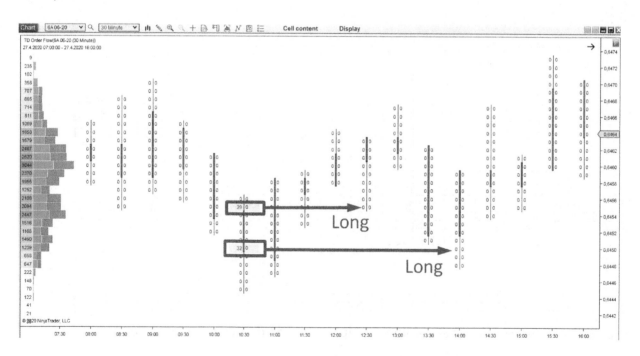

Example #3: Trades Filter

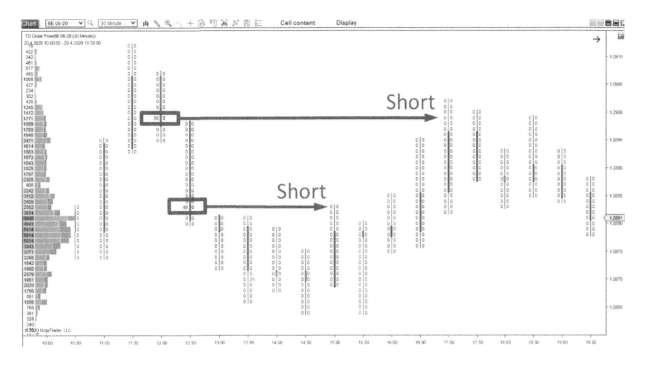

Example #4: Trades Filter

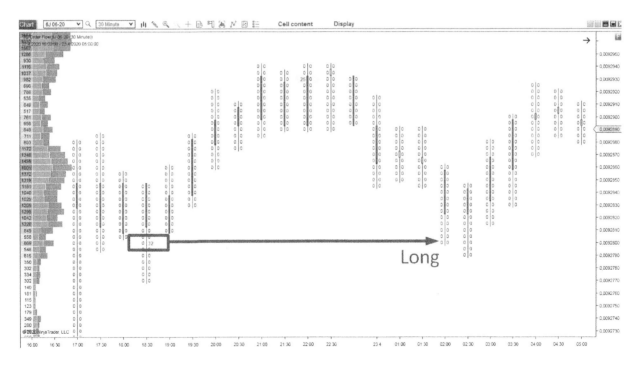

Example #5: Trades Filter

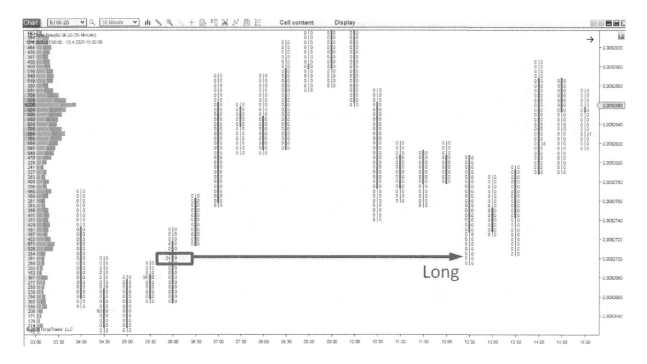

Example #6: Trades Filter

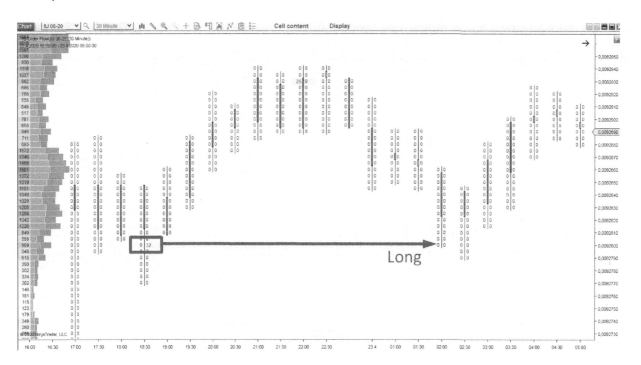

Trading setup #4: Stacked Imbalances

An Imbalance means that one side of the market is way stronger than the other. Either the Buyers are way stronger than the Sellers or the Sellers are much stronger than the Buyers.

This "strength" is measured by comparing the Bid and Ask. The default setting of my software is that if Bid is 300% or more than the Ask, it is marked (in blue color) as Selling Imbalance. If the Ask is 300% or more than the Bid, it is a Buying Imbalance (also in blue).

Selling Imbalances often occur in a downtrend and Buying Imbalances often show in an uptrend.

Selling Imbalances occur at the Bid; Buying Imbalances occur at the Ask.

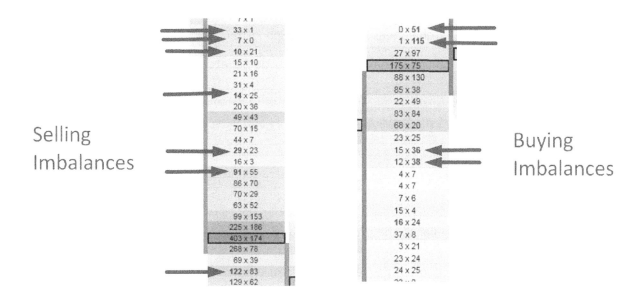

You have the option to turn on/off the imbalances as well as change the trigger percentage in my Order Flow software settings.

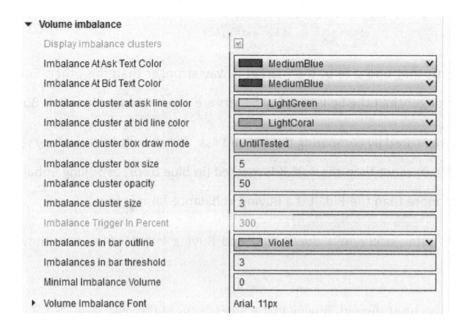

If there are multiple Stacked Imbalances on top of each other, this represents a strong Support/Resistance zone. It indicates that either Buyers or Sellers were really active and strong at this place. It also implies that when the price comes back into this area again, it is likely that those Strong Buyers/Sellers will become active again. We can expect that there will be a reaction.

The way to trade this is very similar to the previous setups:

1. Set your Order Flow to show Bid x Ask. Make sure you have the Imbalances turned "on" in the Indicator settings.

2. If there are more than three Buying or Selling Imbalances stacked on top of each other (default setting, which you can change), then it represents a Stacked Imbalance and this zone will automatically get highlighted. A Support zone created by Stacked Buying Imbalances gets highlighted in green. A Resistance zone created by Stacked Selling Imbalances gets highlighted in red.

3. You need to see the price move away from these highlighted areas first, making at least one or two whole footprints (candles) above or below it. I like to use the 30 Minute footprint chart for this.

4. Then you need to wait for a pullback. When the price returns back to this Stacked Imbalance zone, then you enter your trade.

5. If the price hit this zone from above, then you enter Long. If it makes a pullback from below, then you go Short. An area highlighted in red = Resistance. An area highlighted in green = Support.

6. Trade only the first hit (first test). Don't attempt to trade one trading level more than once as the probability of a second successful reaction to the same level is much lower.

7. It is best to look for Stacked Imbalances within a trend or before a trend begins. Additionally, it does not need to be a strong trend; a strong one-way price movement will do.

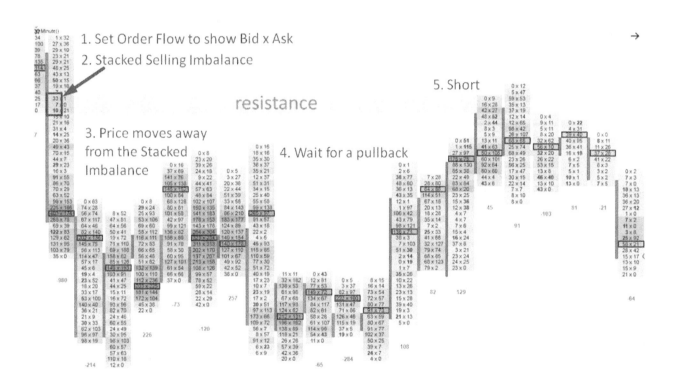

EXAMPLES: Stacked Imbalances

Example #1: Stacked Imbalances

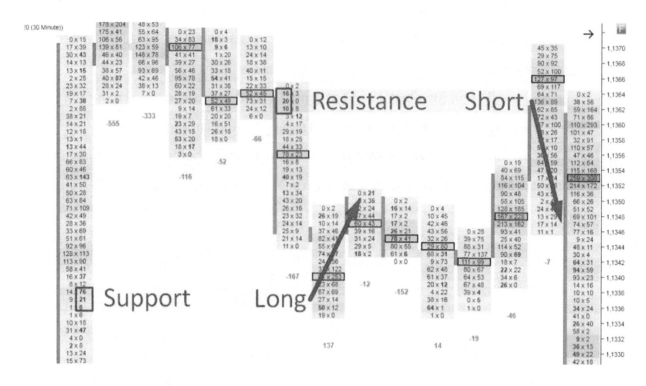

Example #2: Stacked Imbalances

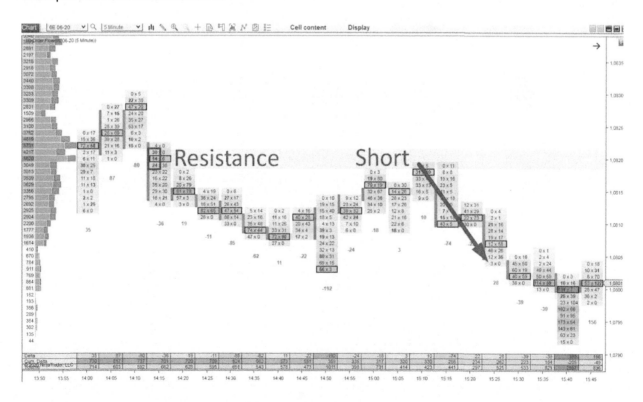

Example #3: Stacked Imbalances

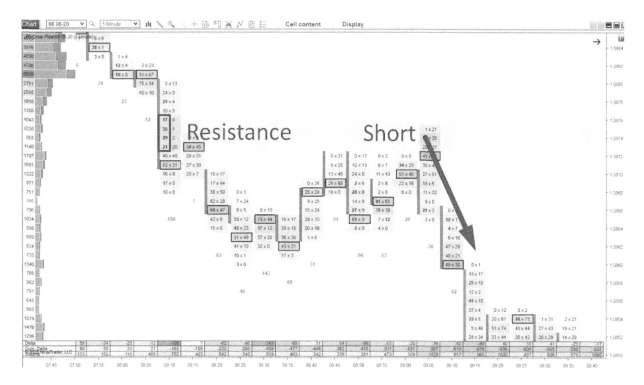

Example #4: Stacked Imbalances

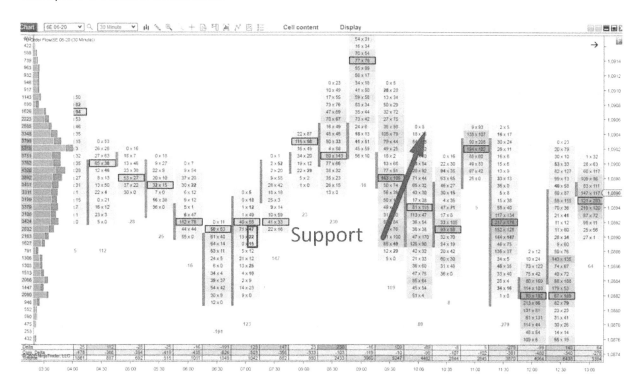

Example #5: Stacked Imbalances

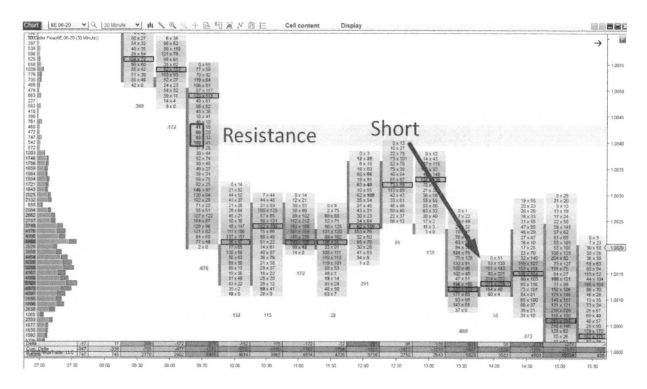

Example #6: Stacked Imbalances

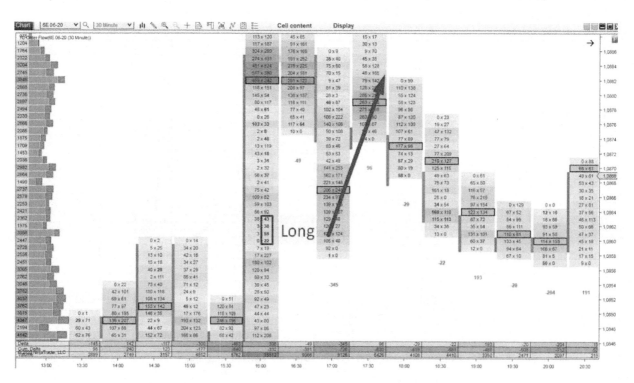

Trading setup #5: Unfinished Business

Unfinished Business represents a market imperfection. It shows that when the price changed its direction, the high or low it created did not form properly.

There is an Auction process when a new high/low is formed, and this process needs to end in a certain way. A properly formed high needs to have 0 contracts traded at Bid, and a properly formed Low needs to have 0 contracts traded at Ask.

When the market turns from a new low or high without this happening (Bid AND Ask are both more than 0), it is called an Unfinished Business (or a Failed Auction).

My software makes this easy to spot by drawing a dotted green or red line there:

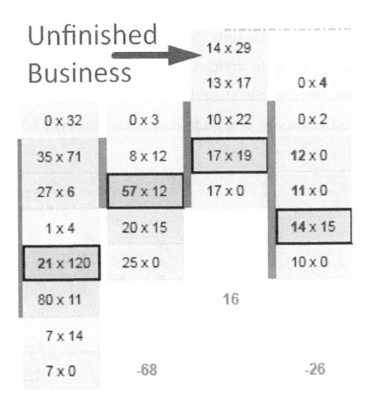

Now I am going to show you a few tips for how you can use Unfinished Business. I don't have a trading setup based solely on trading Unfinished Business; instead, I use it primarily to support other trade setups.

The main thing to remember about Unfinished Business is that it works like a magnet. The price is drawn towards it, and if it comes close, it is likely to move through it.

So, if Unfinished Business works as a magnet, how do we use this information? There are several ways:

- Take Profit
- Stop Loss
- Confirmation
- Warning against bad trades

Take Profit

If you are in a profitable trade and you are thinking about taking your profit, you can check if the price is moving towards Unfinished Business. If it is, then you might remain in your position a little bit longer until the price tests the Unfinished Business—because it should work as a magnet. This can help you to stretch your Take Profit by a few pips. Be careful, though, as there is no guarantee the market will test the Unfinished Business if it is too far away. This technique for extending your take profit works best if the price is already close to the Unfinished Business.

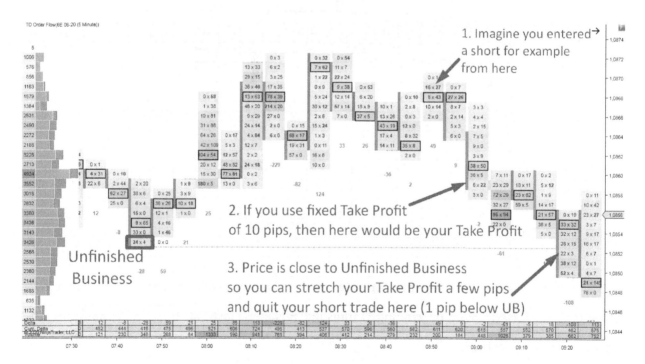

I was using this method in a live trading video, which you can find on the webpage I made for you (https://www.trader-dale.com/of-book/)

This particular video is called "LIVE: Trading JPY Futures - Trailing Position and Delta Divergence."

Stop Loss

When you are deciding where to place your Stop Loss, bear in mind that Unfinished Business works like a magnet. If you place your SL in a way that the Unfinished Business is behind it, then if the price comes close to your SL, it will most likely shoot past it—to test the Unfinished Business.

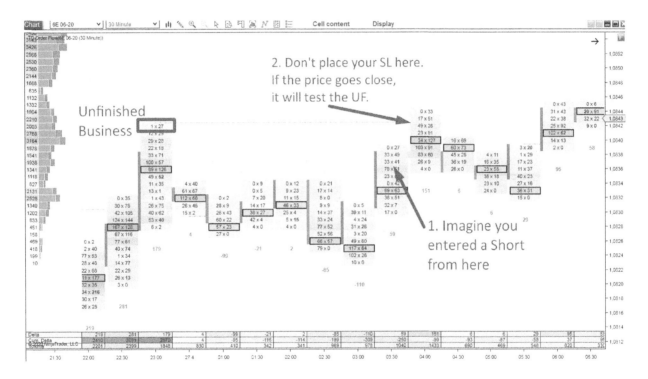

I am not saying I always stick to these rules regarding the Unfinished Business as this is not my main trading strategy. I use Unfinished Business mostly to read the charts, feel what is going on, and make the best picture of what I expect to occur. No trade is perfect, and there will always be something you won't like. But you need to weigh the pros and cons and decide in the end whether the trade is worth taking the risk.

Confirmation

Bearing in mind that Unfinished Business works as a magnet, you can also use it to confirm a trend. Imagine you are in a Long position and the price goes upwards but then it reverses and it starts going against you. Unfinished Business can help you identify whether this is most likely just a pullback or if this is a change of a trend. If you see Unfinished Business at the top of the reversal, then the price probably turned temporarily. It will likely continue upwards again to test the Unfinished Business (magnet).

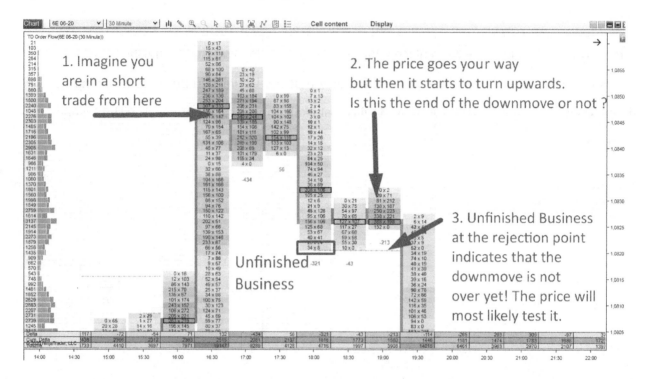

I also used this approach in the live trading session video called "LIVE: Trading JPY Futures - Trailing Position and Delta Divergence." (https://www.trader-dale.com/of-book/)

Warning against Entering a Bad Trade

The Unfinished Business can also warn you against entering a bad trade. Again, the logic is that Unfinished Business works as a magnet, and if the price comes close, it will most likely test it.

Simply put, you don't want to enter a Long trade when there is the Unfinished Business below and you don't want to enter a Short trade when there is the Unfinished Business above your entry.

Why? Because Unfinished Business works as a magnet, and by entering such a trade you would risk the price shooting past your trade entry to test the Unfinished Business.

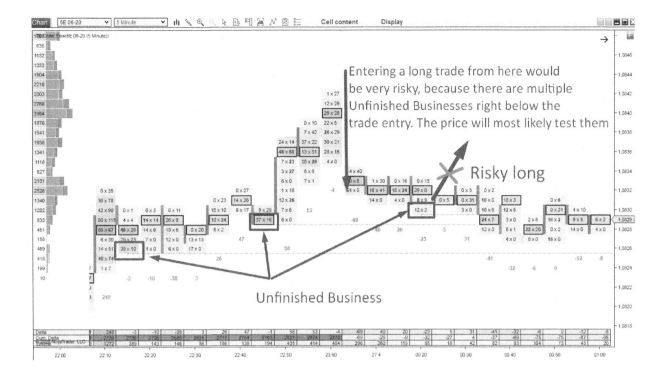

Below are some more examples of Unfinished Business. Notice how the price has the tendency to hit those areas and fix the market imperfection that Unfinished Business represents.

EXAMPLES: Unfinished Business

Example #1: Unfinished Business

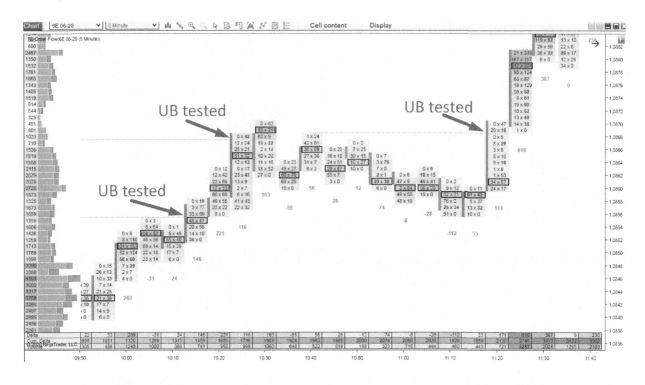

Example #2: Unfinished Business

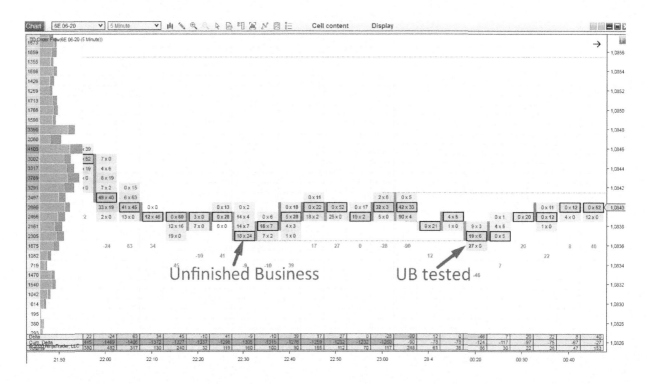

Example #3: Unfinished Business

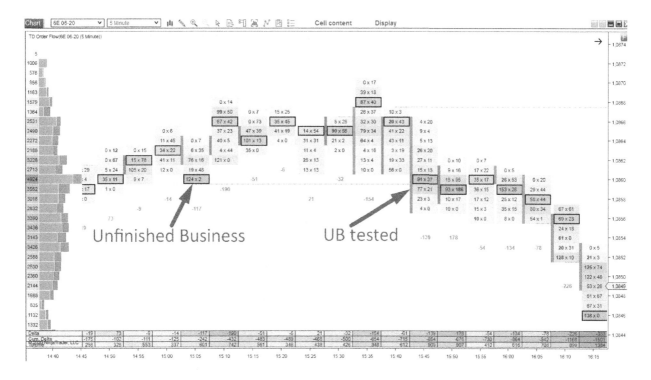

Example #4: Unfinished Business

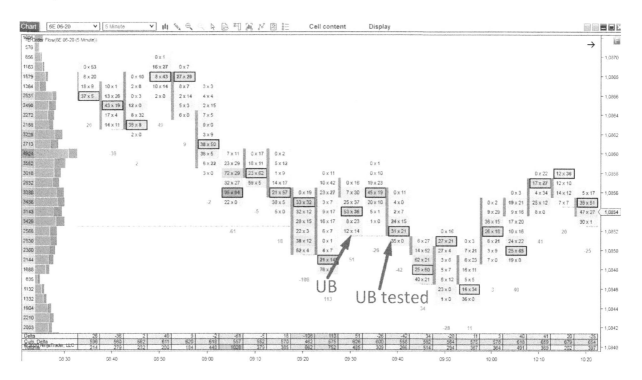

Example #5: Unfinished Business

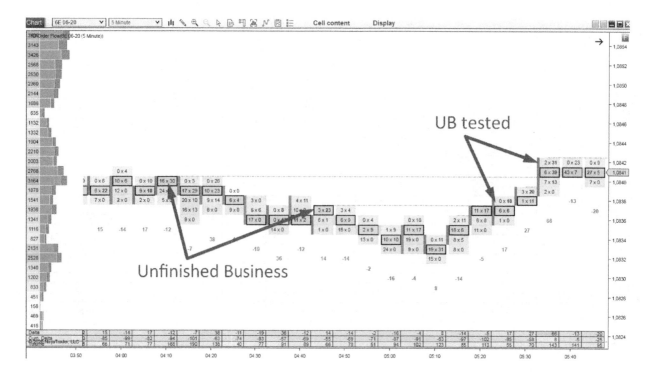

Example #6: Unfinished Business

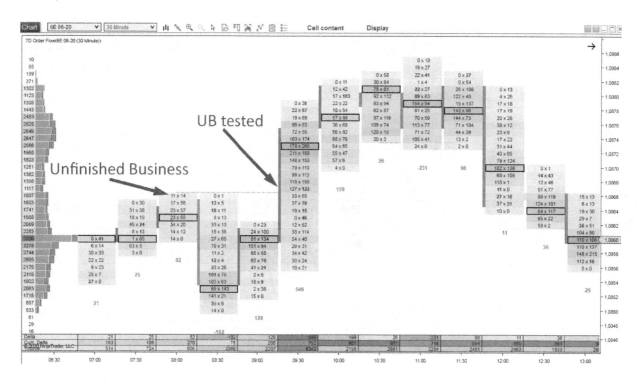

Example #7: Unfinished Business

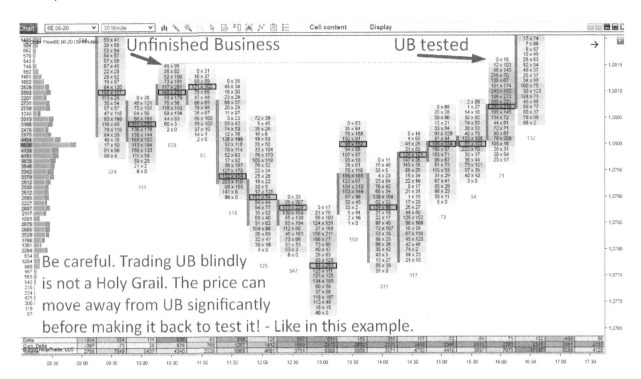

Even though I spent quite a lot of space talking about various uses of Unfinished Business, I would still advise you to focus on the other setups first. Those are standalone and proven trading setups. Unfinished Business is something extra—a bonus. It is an approach that only helps you read the market and helps with your decision-making. Your trading should be based on other strategies, and Unfinished Business should be used as an addition to that.

Order Flow – Confirmations

Confirmation setups are not standard trading setups. You should not base your trading strategy on them alone. Their strength lies in giving you a hint when the market is starting to react to a Support/Resistance zone you found using one of your main trading setups. That would be a setup based on Volume Profile or one of the setups I showed you in the previous chapter.

This is how it works:

First, go through the chart and identify the Support and Resistance zones. You can do this with Volume Profile, Order Flow main setups, or identify S/R zones another way you are familiar with.

After that, mark those S/R zones in your chart. Then wait until the price makes it there. When it does, switch to Order Flow, and wait for a confirmation.

It is important to note that Support and Resistance are ZONES, NOT EXACT levels. When the price reaches such a zone, you want to see a confirmation there, somewhere within that zone. Such a confirmation tells you that the BIG guys (institutions) are starting to react there.

There are four confirmations I like to use. These can give you the final push to enter your trade.

I also like to use these confirmations when I am unsure whether or not to take a trade. This can be, for example, because the price moves very quickly and aggressively against my trading level or the trading level is not really clear (not clear where exactly to place it). I also use confirmations when my trading level is not particularly strong and I am not sure whether to trade it or not.

In all such situations, Order Flow confirmation can help you decide whether to take the trade or skip it.

There are four confirmations I look for when the price reaches a significant Support or Resistance zone. I look for: Big Limit Orders, Absorption, a sign of Aggressive Buyers/Sellers, and confirmation on the Cumulative Delta.

Confirmation Setup #1: Big Limit Orders

When the price reaches a strong Support/Resistance zone, you need to see a sign of a reaction first. This sign could be a BIG institution jumping into the market.

You want to see somebody big who has been waiting around the S/R zone (like you have been) to jump in the trade.

Passive traders who wait for the price to come to them use Limit orders. They don't chase the market with aggressive Market orders. A Limit order is more suitable because they get filled for the price THEY want.

The Limit Confirmation Strategy is quite simple. First, you identify a significant S/R zone (for example, with Volume Profile). Then you wait and look for somebody big to jump in a trade there.

- To get a Resistance zone confirmed, you need to see a Limit Sell order appear.
- To get a Support zone confirmed, you need to see a Limit Buy order appear.

Important: a Limit Sell shows on the Ask and a Limit Buy shows on the Bid.

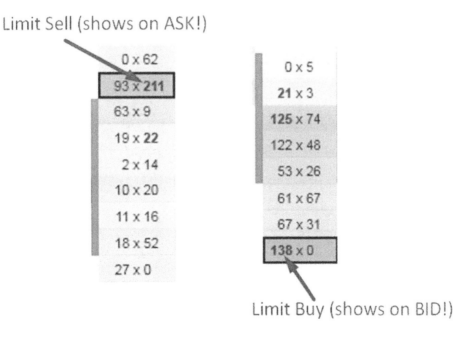

Limit Sell (shows on ASK!)

Limit Buy (shows on BID!)

Steps to Limit Orders Confirmation Setup:

1. Identify a strong Support/Resistance zone using your primary strategy (this could be Volume Profile, Order Flow, Price Action, etc.).

2. When the price gets to that zone, open your Order Flow and wait for a big Limit order (unusually large volumes) to appear. For a Short trade confirmation, you want to see a large number on the Ask. For a Long trade confirmation, it needs to appear on the Bid.

3. I prefer to look for such confirmations on a 5 Minute Bid x Ask Order Flow chart.

4. An important fact to remember is that unusually large volume is different for each trading instrument and each trading session! That's why it is essential to start trading with just one trading instrument. After you have mastered it, only then should you look to add another.

5. Enter your trade as soon as you identify the big Limit order. Sometimes it does not appear all at once, and it may take a few minutes until the whole order is placed.

Below is a EUR Futures, 5 Minute chart showing a Long trade confirmation. If this occurred in a Support zone, it would be a confirmation to enter a Long trade immediately.

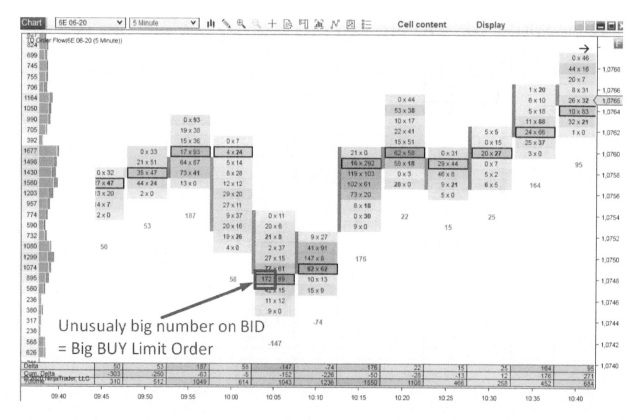

Below is a EUR Futures, 5 Minute chart showing a Short trade confirmation. If this occurred in a Resistance zone, it would be a confirmation to enter a Short trade immediately.

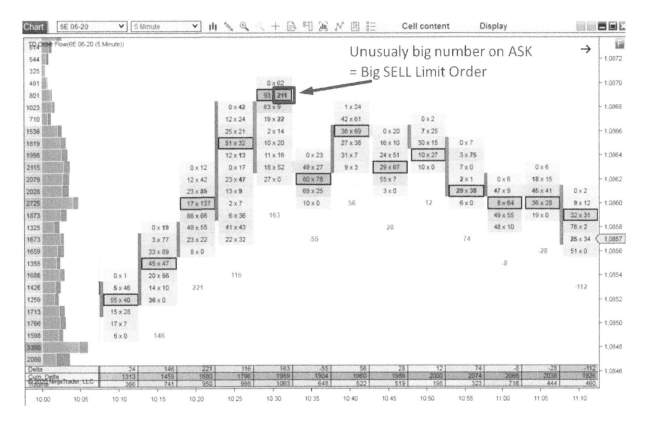

More examples of the Limit order confirmation are below. To reiterate for emphasis, the confirmation must appear around a Support/Resistance zone, NOT just anywhere! I will show you how to identify S/R zones using Volume Profile later in this book.

EXAMPLES: Big Limit Orders

Example #1: Big Limit Orders

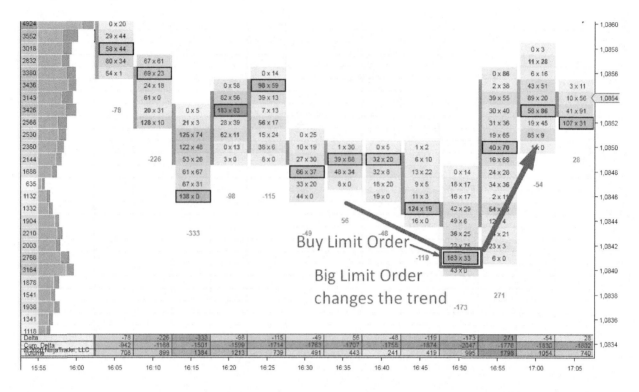

Example #2: Big Limit Orders

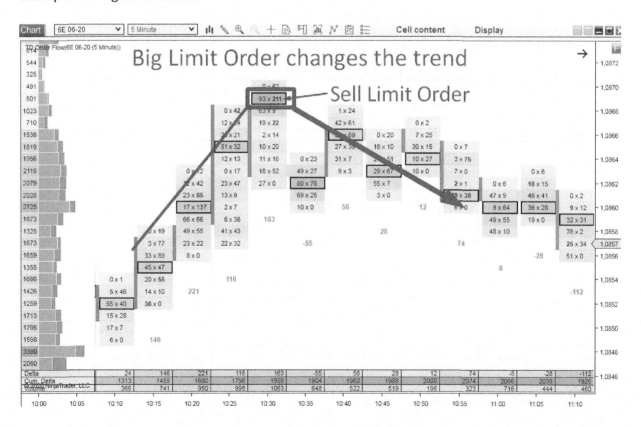

Example #3: Big Limit Orders

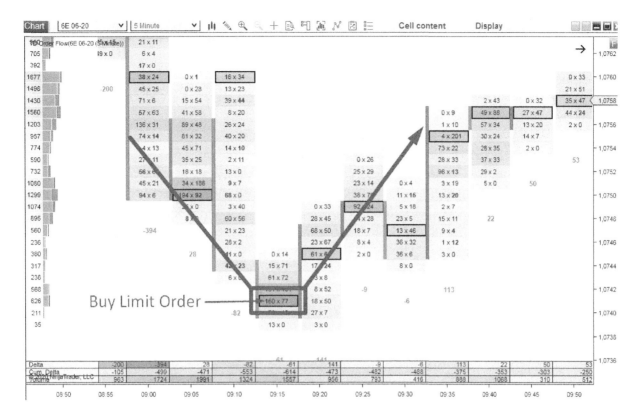

Example #4: Big Limit Orders

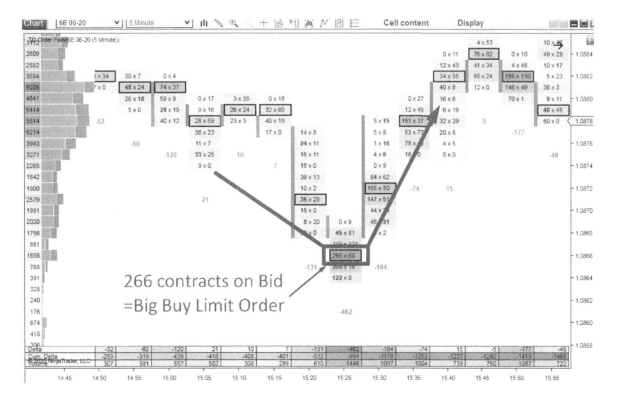

Example #5: Big Limit Orders

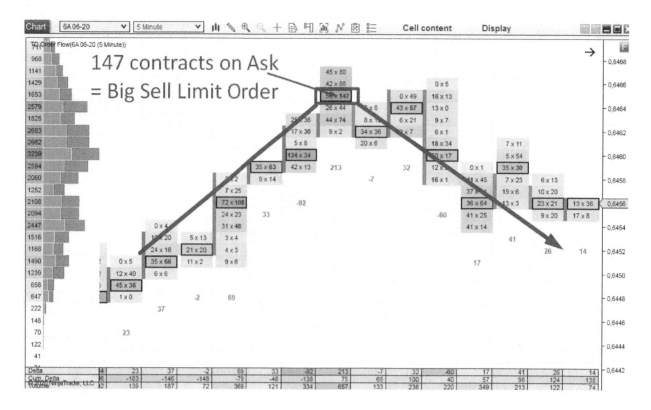

Example #6: Big Limit Orders

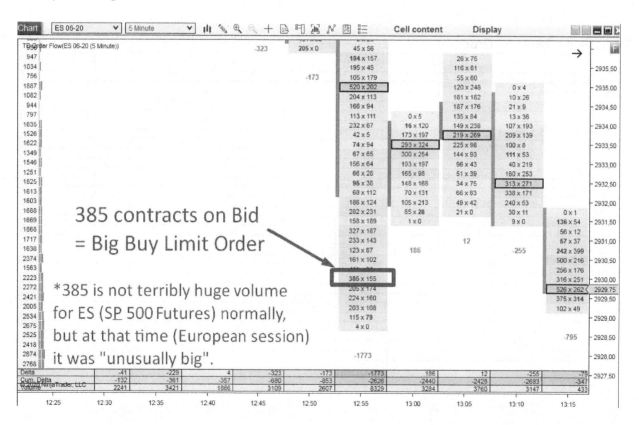

Confirmation Setup #2: Absorption

This confirmation setup is similar to the Limit order setup, only a bit simpler.

In this case, the confirmation you want to see in a Support/Resistance zone is Buyers or Sellers who absorb all the market momentum.

Imagine, for example, that Sellers are pushing the price downwards using aggressive Market Sell orders. But then strong Buyers appear, and they absorb all the selling pressure—all the selling momentum. They buy everything the Sellers are selling. The price does not drop anymore, and heavy volumes start to appear. Those heavy volumes appear on the BID (aggressive Sellers) and ASK (aggressive Buyers).

So, when you see huge volumes traded on the Bid and Ask (both!) around some S/R zone, then it is most likely the Absorption taking place. What is happening there is that the Selling or Buying pressure (momentum) is getting absorbed, making a price reversal likely. That's the confirmation you want to see!

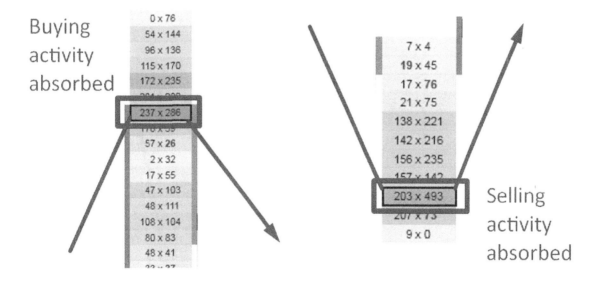

It is also hard to provide an exact definition of the term "unusually large volumes" as they are different for every trading instrument and trading session. With that said, a simple technique you can use is to look at recent Order Flow footprints and determine an average cell volume. An "unusually large" or "huge" volume would be volume way above this average.

An important thing to keep in mind is that this large volume doesn't appear all at once. It can take a while before you can safely tell that the volumes you see jumping in are unusually large compared to the average.

Steps of the Absorption Setup:

1. Identify a strong Support/Resistance zone using your main strategy (this could be Volume Profile strategies, Price Action strategy, etc.).

2. When the price gets near that S/R zone, open your Order Flow chart and wait for unusually heavy volumes to appear on Bid and Ask (both!). The absorption needs to appear around the S/R zone. If it does, then the S/R zone is confirmed.

3. Enter your trade as soon as you identify the Absorption. It may take a few minutes until all the orders on Bid and Ask are placed before you can safely tell that the market is absorbing the Buying/Selling pressure.

I prefer to look for the Absorption on the 5 Minute chart or on a 30 Minute chart.

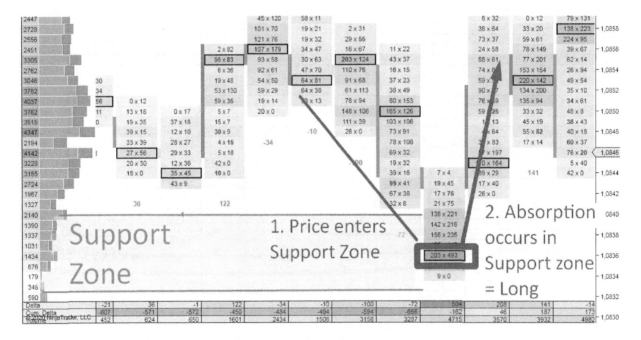

EXAMPLES: Absorption

Example #1: Absorption

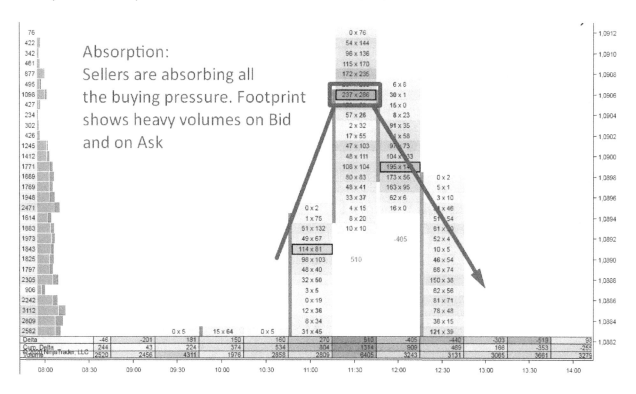

Example #2: Absorption

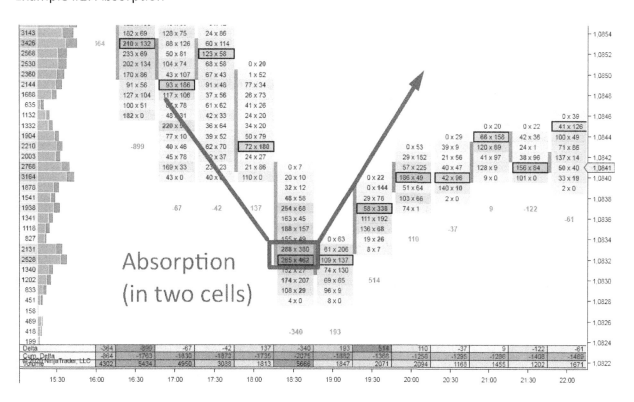

Example #3: Absorption

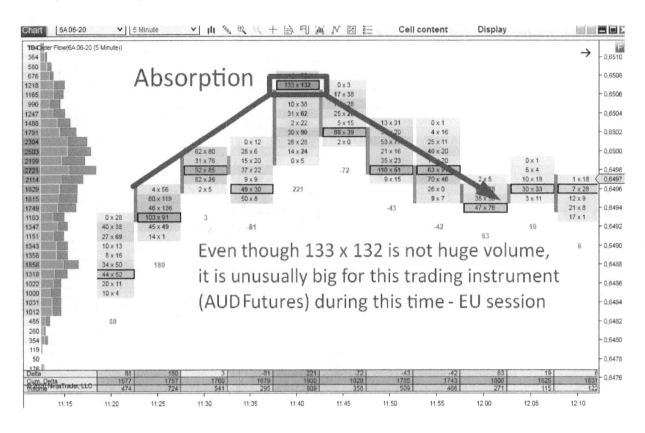

Absorption

Even though 133 x 132 is not huge volume, it is unusually big for this trading instrument (AUD Futures) during this time - EU session

Example #4: Absorption

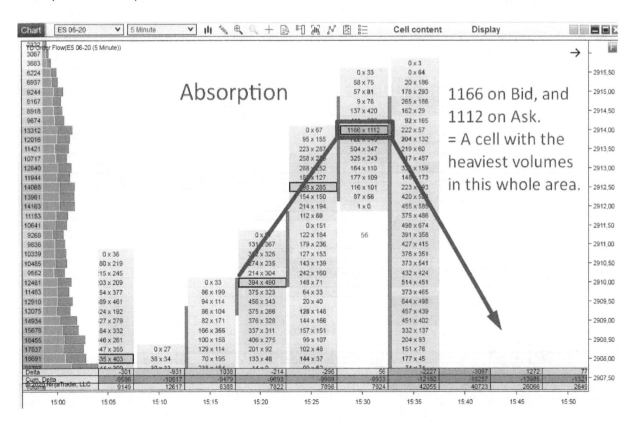

Absorption

1166 on Bid, and 1112 on Ask. = A cell with the heaviest volumes in this whole area.

Example #5: Absorption

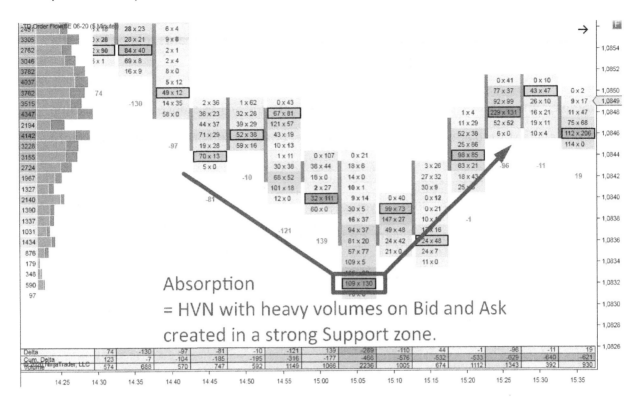

Absorption
= HVN with heavy volumes on Bid and Ask
created in a strong Support zone.

Example #6: Absorption

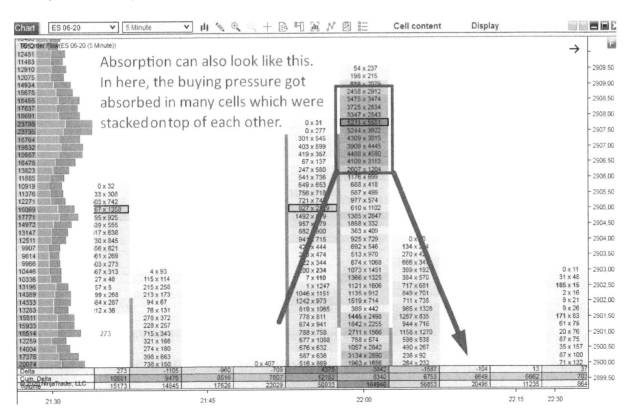

Absorption can also look like this. In here, the buying pressure got absorbed in many cells which were stacked on top of each other.

Confirmation Setup #3: Aggressive Orders and Delta

A really nice confirmation is when you spot aggressive market participants joining the party around a strong Support/Resistance zone.

For example, imagine the price moving upwards, entering a Resistance zone, and then aggressive Sellers start to appear. This is a typical indication that the price will most likely turn downwards.

If the price enters a Resistance zone and you see big volumes starting to appear on Bid, then it is a confirmation that aggressive Sellers are jumping in.

If the price enters a Support zone and you see big volumes starting to appear on Ask, then it is confirmation that aggressive Buyers are jumping in.

Aggressive Buyers show on Ask and aggressive Sellers show on Bid.

It looks like this:

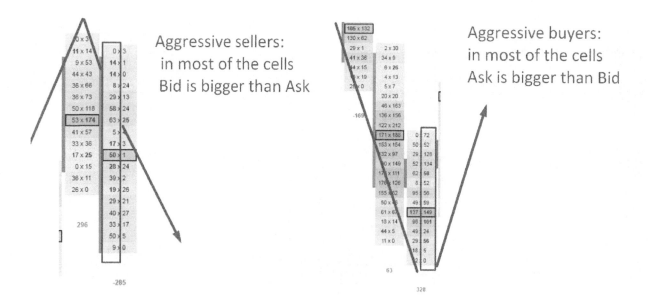

Those aggressive Buyers/Sellers reveal to you that they see the Support/Resistance as well as you do and that they want to trade it. They don't want to miss this trading opportunity. In order not to miss it, they need to enter their trade with a Market order. With a Market order they can be 100% sure their trading order will get filled.

You can look for aggressive Buyers or Sellers by reading individual cells within each footprint (for this, I prefer 5 Minute footprints). Another way to get a quick picture of what is going on in the footprint is the Delta.

Delta

Delta shows a sum of Bid and Ask for each footprint.

If the Delta below the footprint is negative, then more volumes were traded at the Bid. This means that aggressive Sellers dominated in that given footprint. The opposite goes for a positive Delta. A positive Delta tells us that there were more volumes traded on the Ask and that aggressive Buyers dominated that footprint.

Delta shows below each footprint with my Order Flow indicator either as a negative red number or as a positive green number.

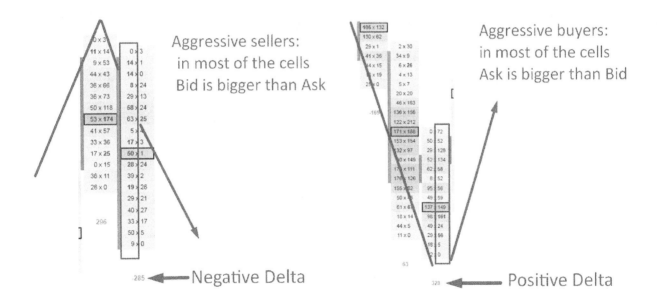

Steps to Aggressive Orders + Delta Setup:

1. Identify a strong Support/Resistance zone using your main strategy (this could be a Volume Profile strategy, Price Action, etc.).

2. When the price gets near that S/R zone, open your Order Flow chart (with Bid x Ask cell content and 5 Minute time frame) and look for aggressive orders.

   If the price entered a Resistance zone, you want to see aggressive Sell orders (way larger volumes on the Bid than the Ask). If the price reached Support, you want to see aggressive Buy orders (way larger volumes on the Ask as compared to the Bid).

   If Bid grows bigger than Ask or the other way around, it will also show on the Delta. It means that aggressive Buyers or Sellers started to jump in.

   For a Short trade confirmation, you want to see a negative Delta. For a Long trade confirmation, you want to see a positive Delta.

3. When you recognize that aggressive Buyers or Sellers have started to jump in and confirmed your Support/Resistance zone, you can immediately enter your trade.

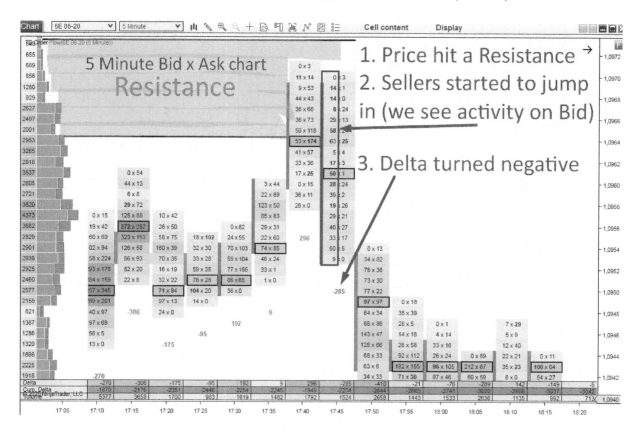

BONUS: Confirmation #1 or #2 Combined with Confirmation #3

The best scenario you can ask for is when there is a combination of two confirmations. The first confirmation you will see is either confirmation #1 (Limit order) or confirmation #2 (Absorption). The confirmation that comes after is the one I have just shown you—the "Aggressive orders" confirmation.

This basically means that some large passive market participant was waiting for the Support/Resistance to get hit. Then this big guy jumped in (Limit order or Absorption), which caused a snowball effect and more people started to join in, this time more aggressively (with Market orders) as they did not want to miss the opportunity.

Here is an example:

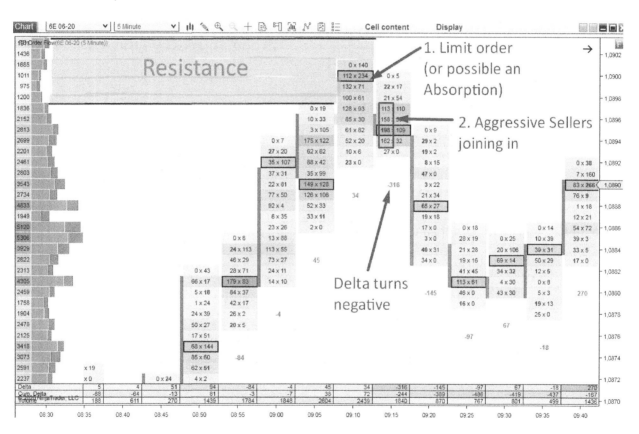

EXAMPLES: Aggressive Orders and Delta

Example #1: Aggressive Orders and Delta

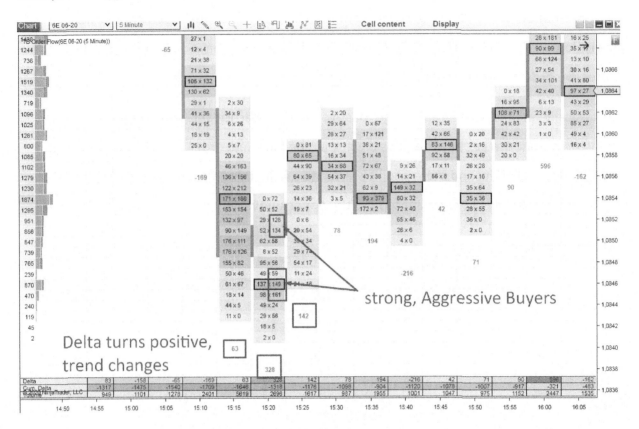

Example #2: Aggressive Orders and Delta

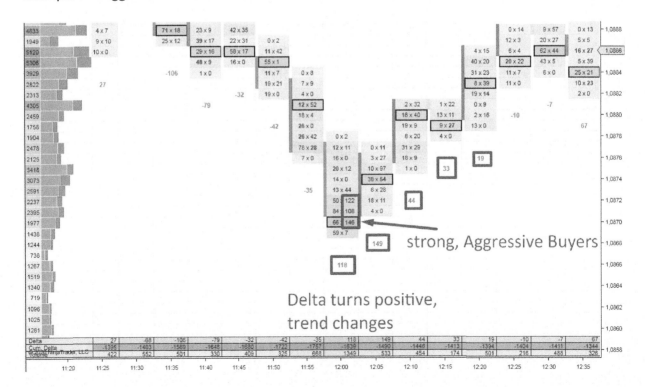

Example #3: Aggressive Orders and Delta

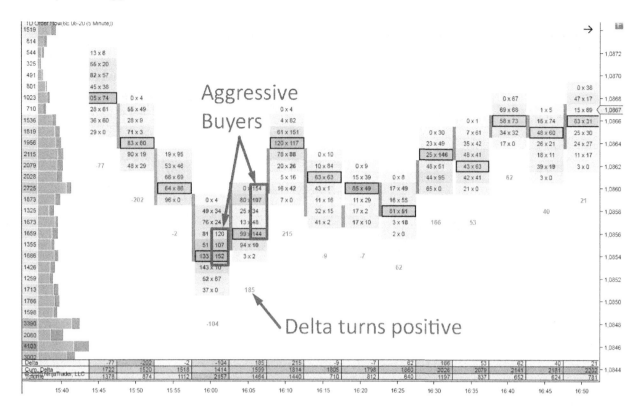

Example #4: Aggressive Orders and Delta

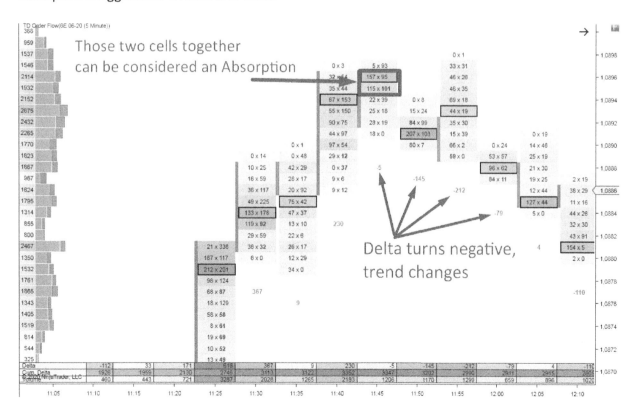

Example #5: Aggressive Orders and Delta

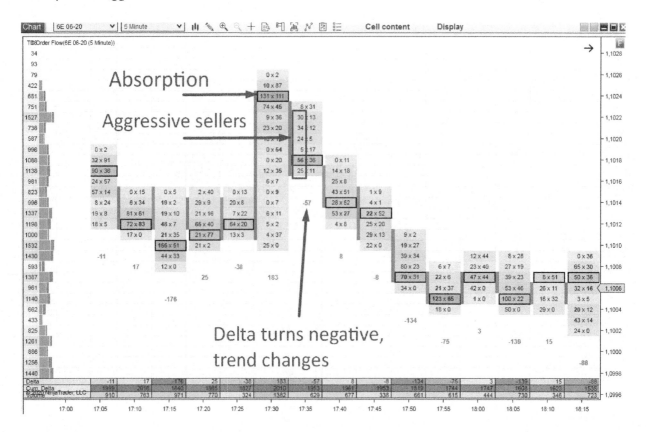

Confirmation Setup #4: Cumulative Delta Divergence

Before I describe this strategy, let me first tell you the distinction between Delta and Cumulative Delta.

Delta = Ask – Bid.

Simply put, Delta is the difference between Buyers and Sellers in each footprint.

Cumulative Delta is a sum of all Deltas since the beginning of the day. For example, if the 1st footprint has Delta = 30, the 2nd footprint has Delta = 100, and the 3rd footprint has Delta = -50, then by the time the 3rd footprint finishes printing, the Cumulative Delta will be +80 (30+100-50).

Here is an example:

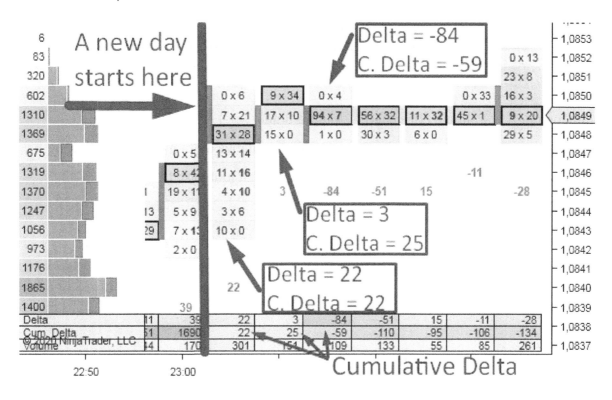

As you can see in the picture above, the Order Flow software automatically calculates the Cumulative Delta in the summary panel below the chart. This is a standard feature included with most Order Flow software.

However, there is an easier way to display the Cumulative Delta. In my Order Flow software, you can print Cumulative Delta on a 1 Minute line chart, and this is how it looks:

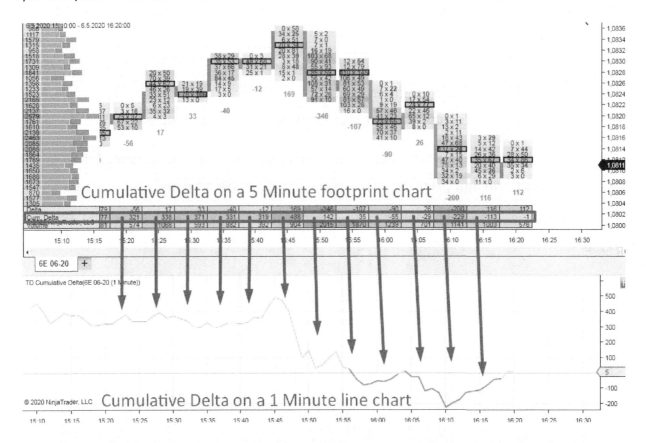

I recommend opening a simple Price chart (1 Minute time frame) atop the Cumulative Delta line chart. This way, you can easily compare price and Cumulative Delta movement, allowing you to spot divergences between the two much more easily. It looks like this:

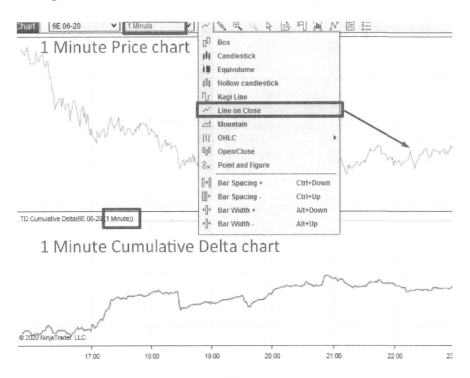

Let's now talk about the strategy I like to use with the Cumulative Delta!

Strategy Description

This strategy is a confirmation strategy—I use it only around strong Support/Resistance zones to confirm my trade entries. I do not use it as a standalone strategy (even though I know people who quite successfully use it this way).

A significant advantage of this strategy is that it is straightforward to interpret and, therefore, very easy to use. Its simplicity and reliability is the reason why it's so popular among my students.

Steps to Cumulative Delta Confirmation Setup:

1. Identify a strong Support/Resistance zone using your primary strategy (this could be a Volume Profile strategy, Price Action, etc.).

2. When the price gets near that S/R zone, open your Cumulative Delta line chart (it is a separate indicator in NinjaTrader 8 platform). Use it together with the 1 Minute Price chart.

3. Wait for a divergence between Price and Cum. Delta to appear and then enter your trade.

For a Short trade confirmation, you want to see the price heading upwards whilst Cumulative Delta is heading down. This tells you that, even though the price is heading up, there is more activity on the Bid (possibly Sellers) and that the price should turn downwards eventually—to correspond with the dropping Cumulative Delta.

For a Long trade confirmation, you want to see the price heading downwards while Cumulative Delta is heading up. This tells you that, even though the price is going down, there is more activity on Ask (possibly Buyers) and that the price should turn upwards eventually— to correspond with the rising Cumulative Delta.

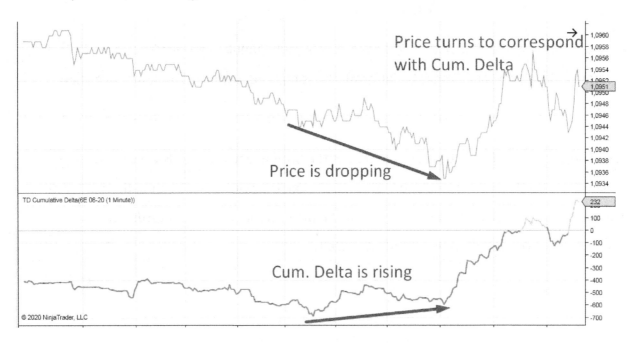

Here are some more examples of Price and Cumulative Delta divergence. If something like this appears around an S/R zone, it is a confirmation to enter your trade.

Example #1: Cumulative Delta Divergence

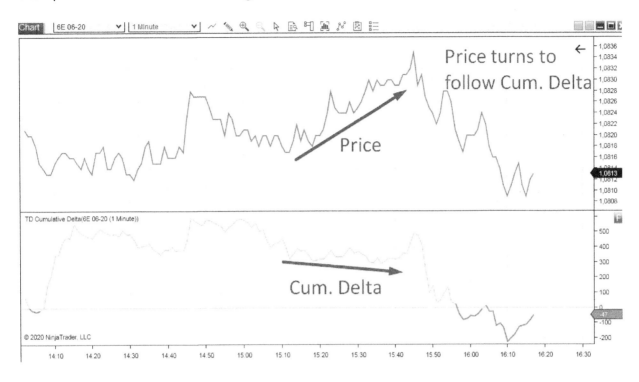

Example #2: Cumulative Delta Divergence

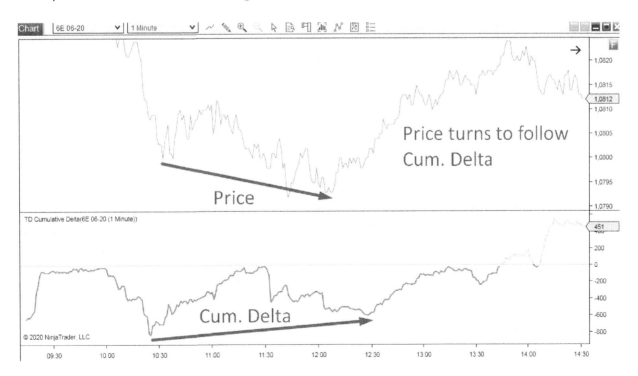

Example #3: Cumulative Delta Divergence

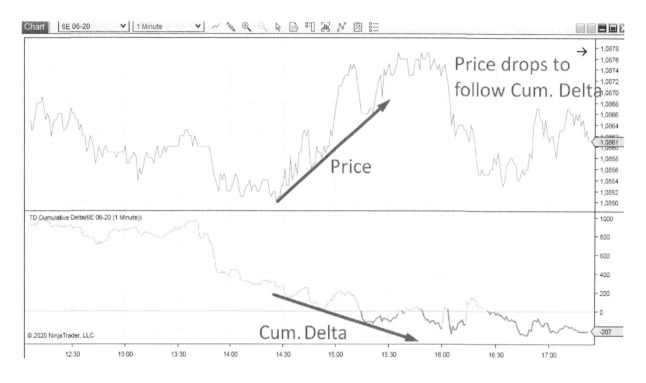

Example #4: Cumulative Delta Divergence

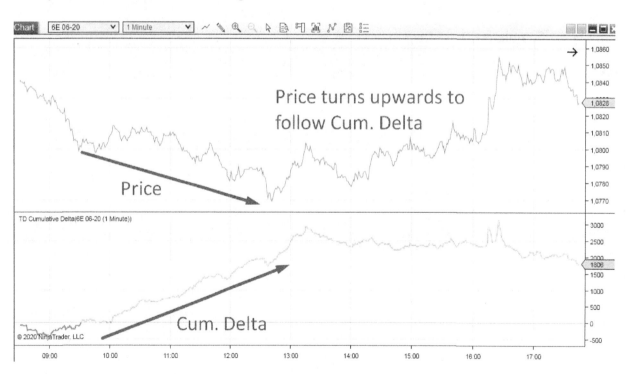

Take Profit with Order Flow

In this chapter, I am going to talk about using Order Flow to determine when and where to quit your winning trade. Order Flow is a very useful tool as it allows you to identify a good Take Profit, helps you maximize your gain and assists in trailing your position. It can also warn you in advance if there is an impending risk that the market could turn against you.

Volume-Based Take Profit

Let me start by pointing out the most important message you should remember from this chapter: <u>Take your profit in a heavy volume area.</u>

The reason for this is that heavy volume areas often work as Support and Resistance zones. Whenever the price reaches a Support or Resistance zone, there is a risk that it will react to it and turn in the opposite direction. This is the reason why you should take your profit before such risk arises.

<u>Tip #1:</u> It is safer to take your profit a bit sooner—just a little bit before the heavy volume area. This reduces the risk that the market will turn against you at the last moment, causing you to miss your Take Profit. This is because, in my experience, the price sometimes reacts a bit before it actually reaches the heavy volume area.

<u>Tip #2:</u> If the closest heavy volume area is too close to your trade entry and the risk would not be worth it (too small Risk/Reward Ratio), then you have two options. The first option is not to take the trade. The second option is bolder—you take the trade, but you don't quit it when it hits the closest heavy volume area. Instead, you close it just before it hits the next one.

I use 30 Minute footprints to determine which heavy volume zones I should use to close my position. This higher time frame allows me to see the bigger picture, which helps identify heavy volume zones easier.

Since you don't need Bid x Ask data, you can use this Take Profit placement strategy for Forex trading as well.

Here is an example of how to determine a Take Profit for a Short trade:

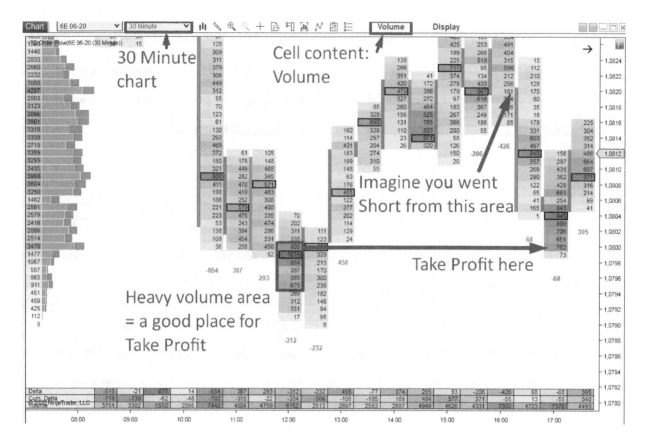

In the picture above, you can see that the ideal volume-based Take Profit would be at 1.0800. This is where heavy volumes were traded before; therefore, this area could work as a Support. When you are in a Short trade, you don't want to risk that the price will react to such Support. The best thing to do is to take your profit just a bit before the price reaches this level. As you can see, the price reacted to this Support and turned upwards. If you didn't close your Short trade when it reached the heavy volume area, this would have ruined it.

EXAMPLES: Volume-Based Take Profit

Example #1: Volume-Based Take Profit

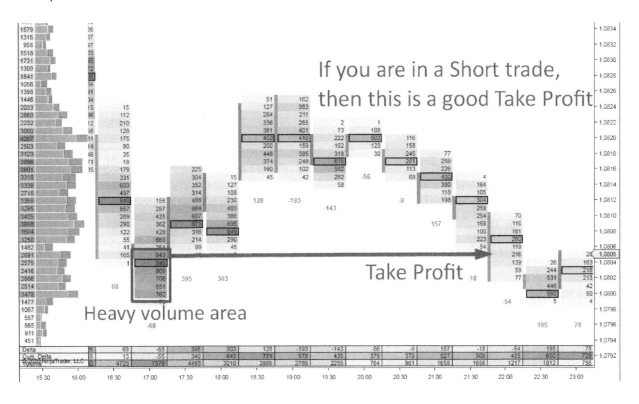

Example #2: Volume-Based Take Profit

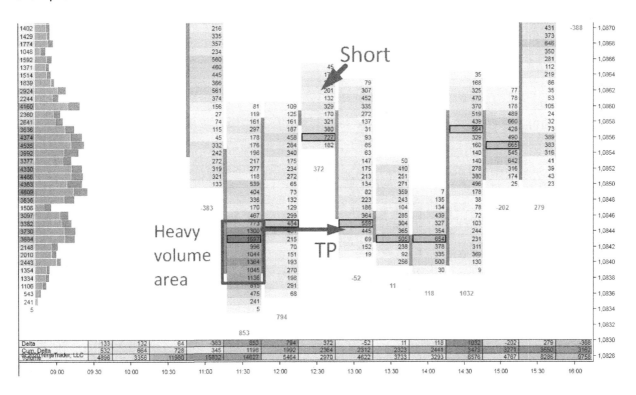

Example #3: Volume-Based Take Profit

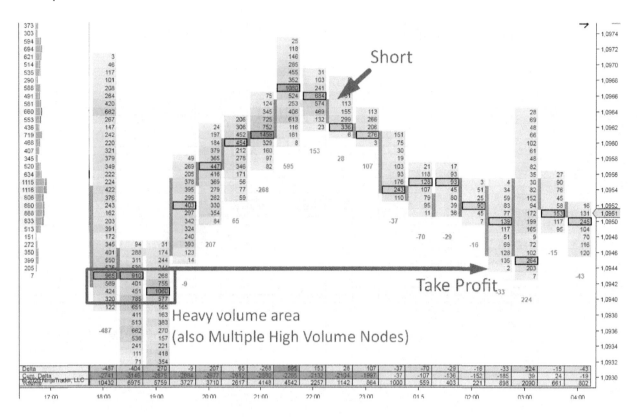

Example #4: Volume-Based Take Profit

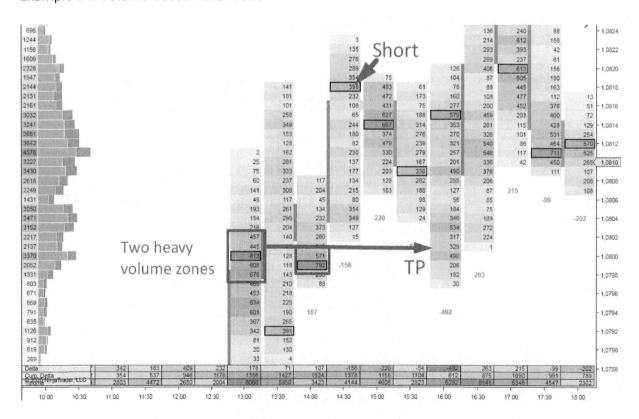

Example #5: Volume-Based Take Profit

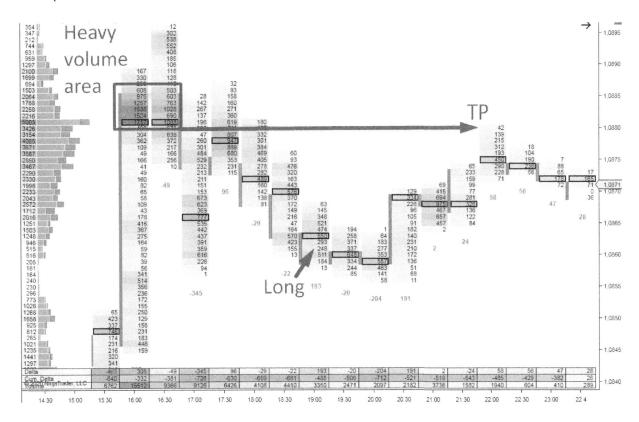

Example #6: Volume-Based Take Profit

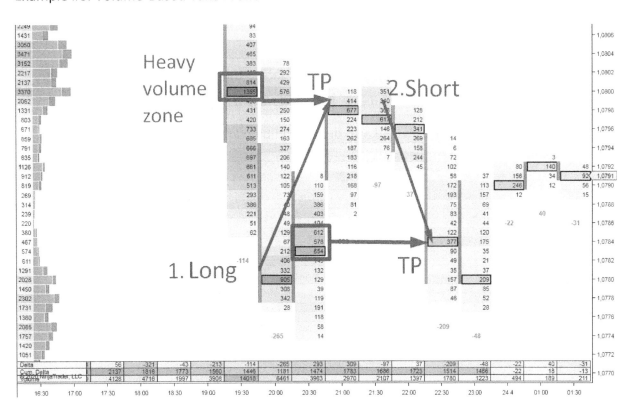

Take Profit – Trailing

For those who like to trail their Stop Loss, this section is for you. Being greedy does not usually pay off in trading, but if you learn this Order Flow technique, it will help you recognize when you can afford to be greedy.

The main idea behind trailing your Stop Loss using Order Flow is to trail it only when you see aggressive market participants on your side.

So, to trail your Long position, you want to see aggressive Buyers. Why quit a Long trade when aggressive Buyers are pushing the price higher and higher, right?

The same, only reversed, goes for a Short position: You can trail your Short if there are aggressive Sellers actively pushing the price downward.

How can you tell if one side of the market is way more aggressive than the other? The easiest way is to look for Imbalances. When you are Long, you want to see Buying Imbalances. When you are Short, you want to see Selling Imbalances.

If the price continues to move rapidly and it creates an Imbalance on the way, then you can trail your position some more.

Imbalance = Sign of aggressive Buyers/Sellers.

*Just to freshen up your memory: If the Bid is 300% or larger than the Ask, then it is a Selling Imbalance. It is marked in blue and shows on Bid. If the Ask is 300% or larger than the Bid, then it is a Buying Imbalance. This would also be marked blue and it shows on Ask.

I like to trail my trades using 5 Minute Bid x Ask footprints:

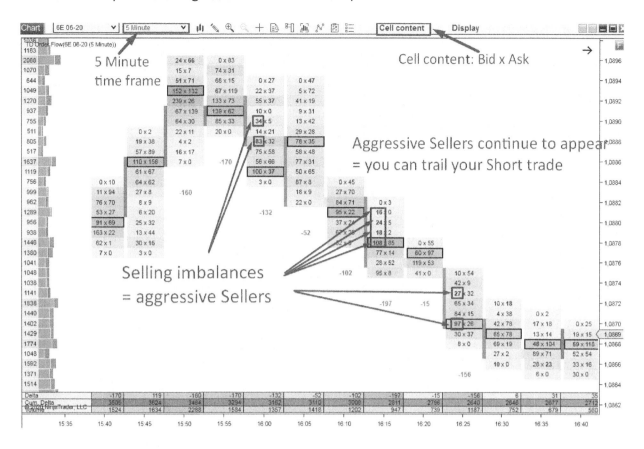

I also use this trailing method in a live trading video, which you can find on the webpage I made for you (https://www.trader-dale.com/of-book/).

This particular video is called "LIVE: Trading JPY Futures - Trailing Position and Delta Divergence."

Trailing TP - Warning Signals

When should you stop trailing your position? It is best to stop trailing your position when you see a warning signal that says the market momentum may have changed. What exactly is the warning signal? It is essentially a trading signal that goes against your position. As an example, imagine you are in a Long position but one of the Order Flow setups says you should now go Short.

Those signals are: **Limit orders, Absorption, Aggressive orders going against you, or a divergence between Price and Delta**. Sounds familiar? Yea—those are the Order Flow setups I showed you before. If you spot any of those setups going against your position, it is high time to quit your trade. This is especially true if you see any of them appear around a strong

level of Support/Resistance or in a heavy volume zone.

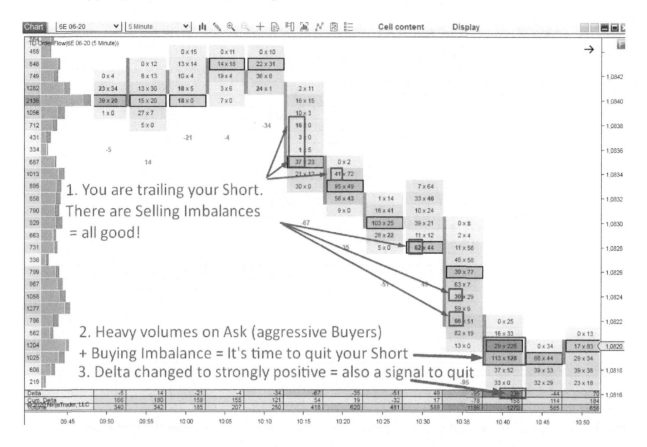

Example #1: Take Profit - Trailing

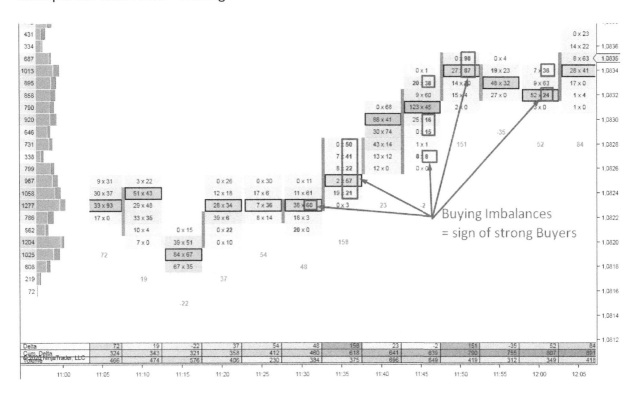

Example #2: Take Profit - Trailing

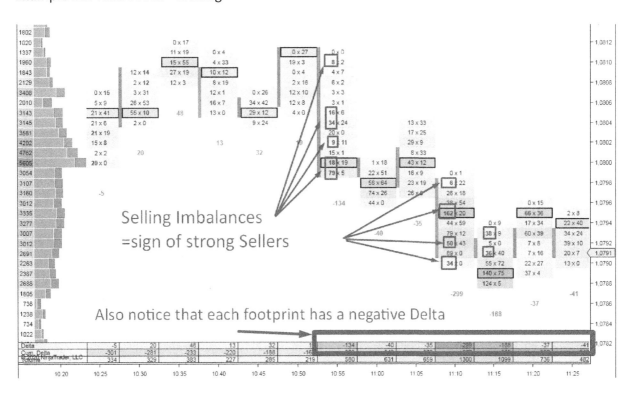

Example #3: Take Profit - Trailing

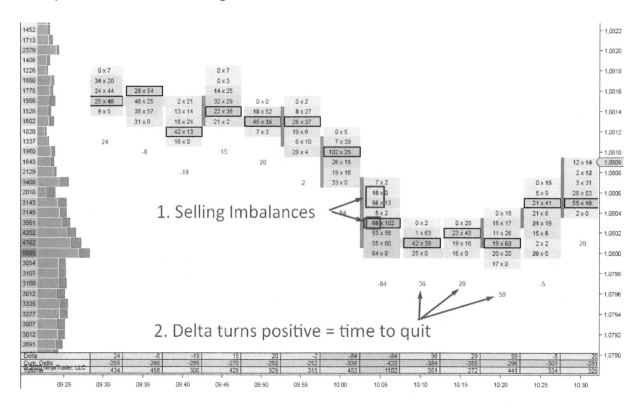

Example #4: Take Profit - Trailing

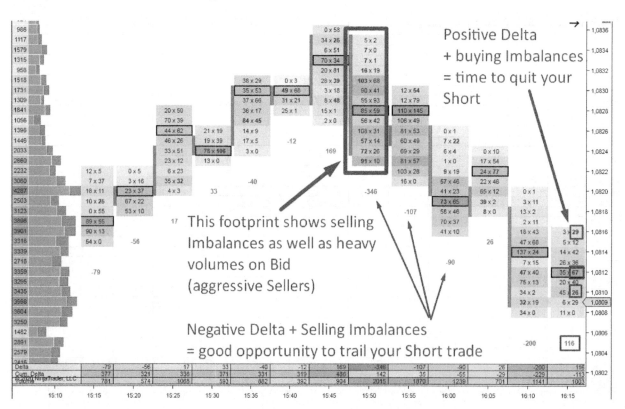

Stop Loss with Order Flow

There are three methods of determining your Stop Loss location.

1. **Fixed SL:** This is the simplest way to place your Stop Loss. It is the simplest because your SL is always the same (for example, 10 pips). For all your trades, you just use the same SL. An advantage of this is that you don't need to think about each trade and its SL separately. A disadvantage is that this method does not adjust to changing market conditions. You can alter this Fixed SL from time to time when the market conditions change dramatically. But still, it is not as flexible and does not reflect the current market conditions as well as the other two approaches.

2. **High/low of the Support/Resistance area:** This means placing your SL at the high/low of the S/R resistance area you are trading. I best explain this using the examples below.

3. **Low volume area:** This means placing your SL in a low volume area, which is located behind a heavy volume area. The reason behind this is that heavy volume areas work as zones of Support/Resistance. The price should not go past them. If it does go past a heavy volume area, then it is a sign of strong market momentum and there is no reason for staying in a trade that would go against that momentum. If a heavy volume zone fails to hold the price and it goes past it into the low volume area, it is time to quit your trade. For this approach, I use the 30 Minute chart with cell content: Volume. I don't need to see Bid x Ask. At this point it is not important whether the volumes were placed at Bid or Ask. What matters here is the total volume.

My preferred time frame for all these three approaches is the 30 Minute TF.

Which of the three approaches to choose though? I suggest you either stick with the first one (Fixed SL) or for each trade you pick one of the two remaining—the second or third depending on the market situation (as there will be scenarios where you will be unable to use one of them).

You always should have some rough idea of how wide your SL should be. With each of these approaches I suggest using your SL somewhere (roughly) within the 10–20% of average daily volatility of the instrument you trade. You can measure the average volatility by ATR indicator (a free indicator is available in every trading platform).

For example, if the average daily volatility of EUR/USD is 100 pips, then you want your SL somewhere (roughly) between 10 and 20 pips. I am not talking just about the first approach here (Fixed SL) but also about the other two. The place which the second or third approach points you to should also be somewhere roughly within the 10–20 pip range. If your SL method points you to a SL that would be outside of this range (either too tight or too wide), then it is best to either skip the trade or use a fixed SL somewhere within the 10–20% range. The reason for this is that it would be crazy having too wide an SL (this would lower your RRR significantly) or one that is too tight (high risk of SL being hit).

What you should aim for is having an SL in a place that makes logical sense and that is also within 10–20% of the daily average range.

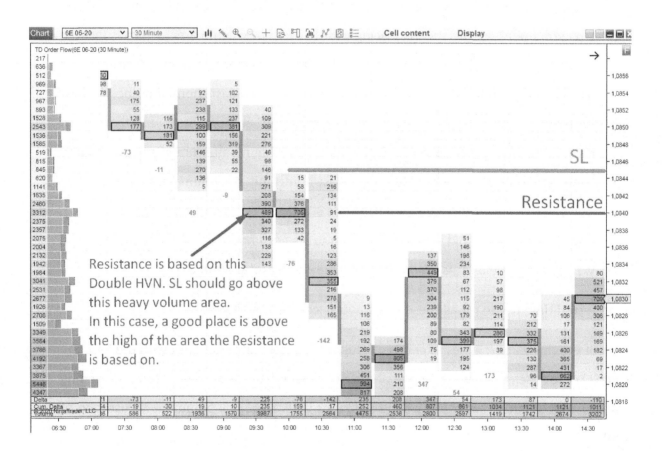

EXAMPLES: Stop Loss with Order Flow

Here are some more examples of SL placement (all based on the second and third approach)

Example #1: SL Placement

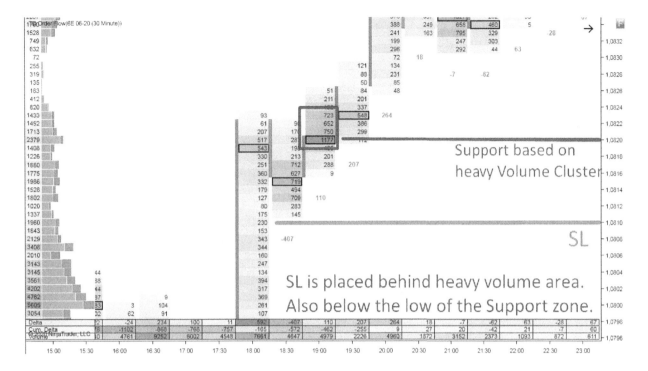

Support based on heavy Volume Cluster

SL

SL is placed behind heavy volume area. Also below the low of the Support zone.

Example #2: SL Placement

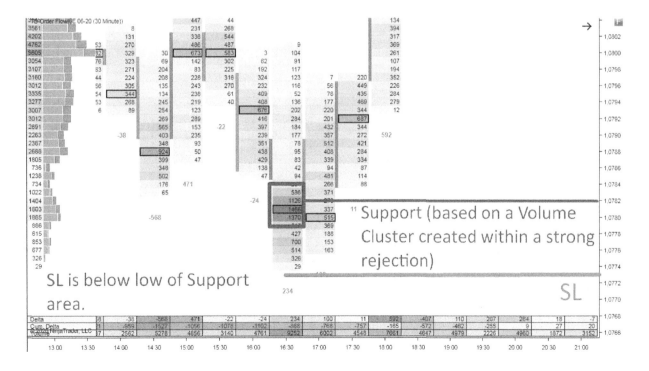

Support (based on a Volume Cluster created within a strong rejection)

SL

SL is below low of Support area.

Example #3: SL Placement

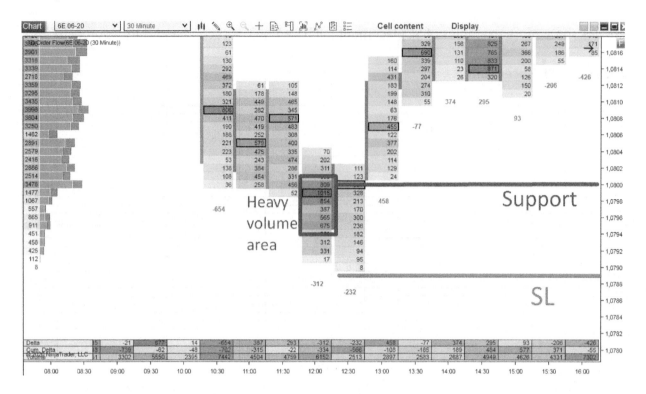

Example #4: SL Placement

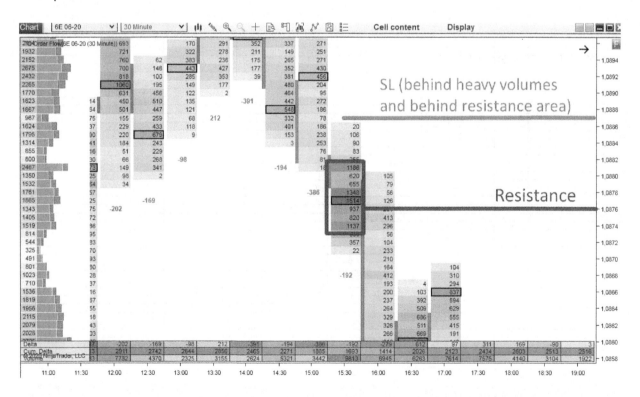

Example #5: SL Placement

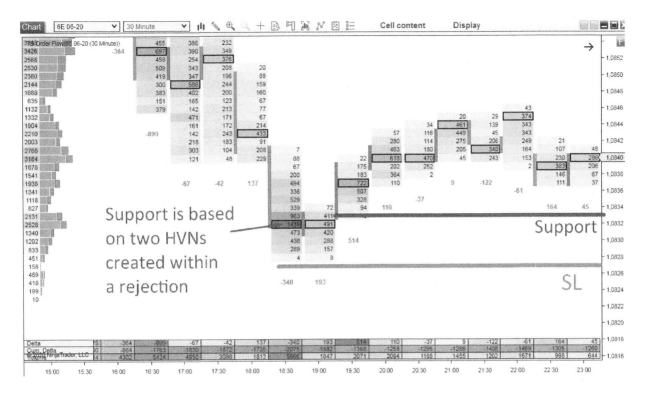

Support is based on two HVNs created within a rejection

Support

SL

Example #6: SL Placement

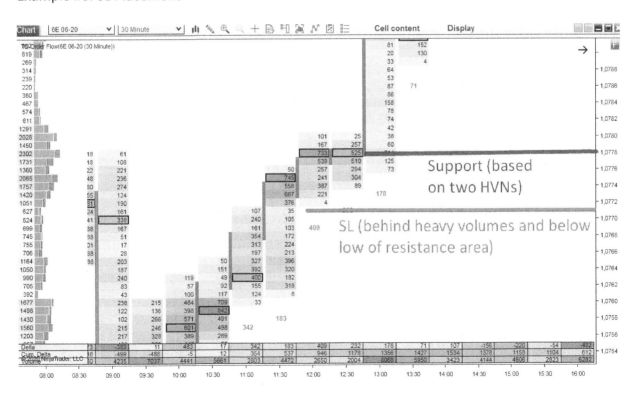

Support (based on two HVNs)

SL (behind heavy volumes and below low of resistance area)

Example #7: SL Placement

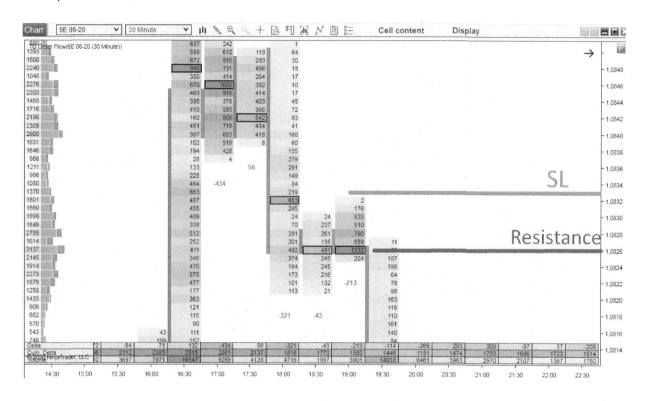

Example #8: SL Placement

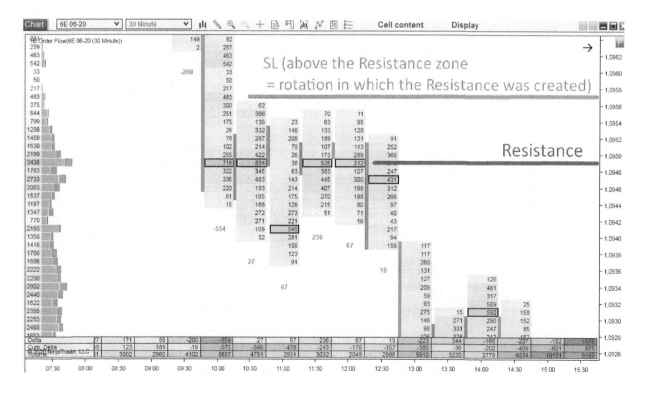

How to Find Supports and Resistances with Volume Profile

Volume Profile Introduction

Order Flow is a fantastic tool that works great if you use it around strong Support and Resistance zones. You can use the Order Flow confirmation strategies to tell whether the price is really reacting to the S/R zone or if the S/R zone is most likely to fail.

In this section, I would like to show you how to identify such strong Support and Resistance zones using my favorite tool—Volume Profile.   ·

Volume Profile is my favorite tool for identifying strong S/R zones because it can show you the bigger picture of what is going on in the chart. This complements the Order Flow, which shows more of the granular detail.

In the next chapters, I am going to teach you the Volume Profile basics and show you my favorite Volume Profile setups. Those are setups that you can use to identify strong S/R zones from which you can later trade using the Order Flow confirmation setups.

VOLUME PROFILE DEFINITION: Volume Profile is a trading indicator that shows Volume at Price. It helps to identify where the big financial institutions put their money and helps to reveal their intentions.

What Does Volume Profile Look Like?

Volume Profile can have many shapes depending on how the volumes get distributed throughout the day. It is created using horizontal lines (it is a histogram). The thicker the profile is the more volume was traded at the given level. If a profile is thin in some places, it means that there was not much volume traded there.

Here is an example of what Volume Profile can look like:

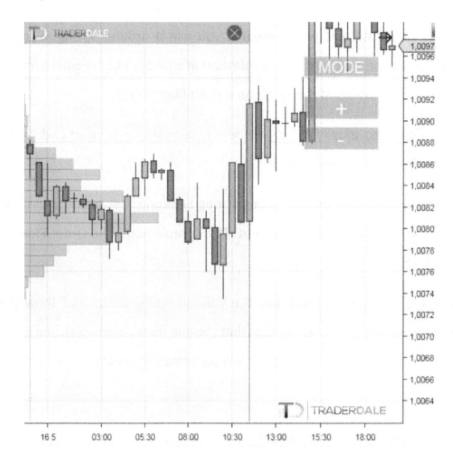

How is Volume Profile Different to Standard Volume Indicators in MT4?

Volume Profile shows volume at price. Standard volume indicators from MT4 (or any other software) show volume during a specific time period.

That is a big difference!

Volume Profile shows you what price levels are important for the big trading institutions. Therefore, it points you to strong Support and Resistance zones.

Standard volume indicators only show WHEN there were big volumes traded. This tells you nothing about essential price levels (Support/Resistance zones).

Here is a picture that compares volume at price (Volume Profile) and volume over a specific time period (standard volume indicator).

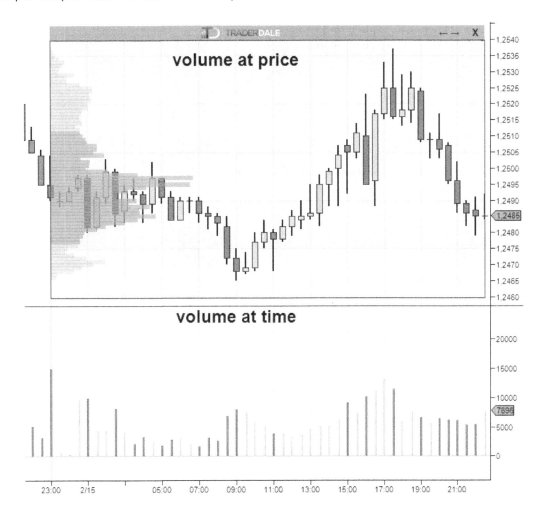

What does Volume Profile Tell Us?

Volume Profile tells us how the volume was distributed over a given price range. This is very useful information. Let me demonstrate with an example.

You can see two heavy volume zones in the picture below and one zone where the Volume Profile is thin.

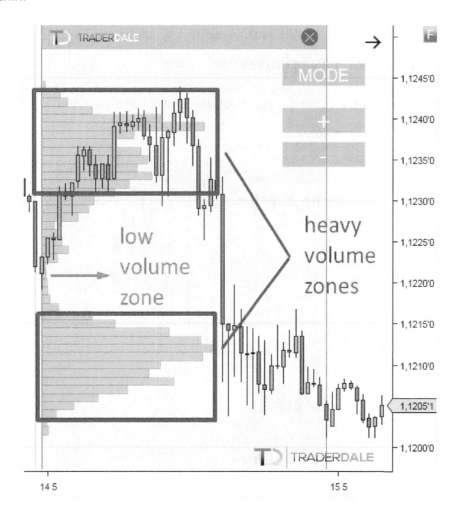

What does this particular picture tell us? It tells us that big financial institutions were interested in trading in those two heavy volume zones. On the other hand, they did not really care for trading too much in the middle zone where the volumes were weak.

This scenario could be a sign that big institutions were:

1. Building up their huge selling positions in the heavy volume zone (1.1230 –1.1240).
2. Manipulating the price to go into a sell-off (that's the thin profile).
3. And, finally, quitting their positions (or adding to them) in the heavy volume zone around 1.1205–1.1215.

Different Volume Profile Shapes

There are many shapes a Volume Profile histogram can print and many different stories it can tell. However, the shapes and the stories behind them tend to repeat themselves, and in the end, it comes down to just a few basic shapes the Volume Profile can take:

D-Shaped Profile

It corresponds with the letter "D" and this is the most common shape. It tells us that there is a temporary balance in the market. Big financial institutions are building up their trading positions and they are getting ready for a big move.

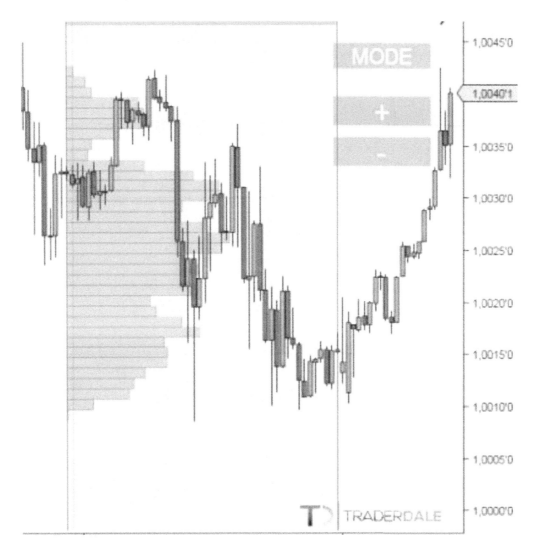

P-Shaped Profile

It corresponds with the letter "P" and this is a sign of an uptrend. Aggressive institutional buyers were pushing the price upwards; then the price found fair value and a rotation started. In this rotation, heavy volumes were traded, and the market was getting ready for the next big move. P-shaped profiles are usually seen in an uptrend or at the end of a downtrend.

b-Shaped Profile

It corresponds with the letter "b" and is the exact opposite of P-shaped profile.

b-shaped profiles are usually seen in a downtrend or at the end of an uptrend.

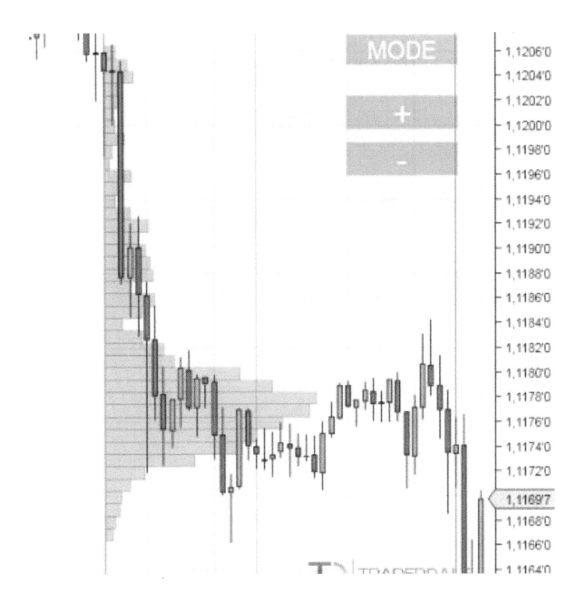

Thin Profile

It corresponds with the letter "I" (with little bumps in it).

A thin profile means a strong trend. There is not much time for building up trading positions in an aggressive price movement. Only small Volume Clusters (sort of "bumps") are created in this kind of profile.

One of my favorite trading strategies is based on those Volume Clusters!

What Makes Volume Profile Different to Other Trading Indicators?

No other indicator (apart from Order Flow, of course) can show you where the big trading institutions were likely buying/selling! Why? Because 99% of all standard indicators are calculated only from two variables: Price and Time. Volume Profile gets calculated using three variables—Price, Time, and Volume.

In other words, 99% of standard trading indicators only show you how the price was moving in the past. The only difference between those thousands of indicators is how they visualize it. It does not matter whether it is EMA, Bollinger bands, RSI, MACD, or any other indicator… All those only show a different visualization of a price movement in the past (they are delayed—they visualize something that has already happened).

YES – they are pretty useless, which is the reason traders keep jumping from one to the other without having any real success.

On the other hand, Volume Profile points you to zones that were and will be important for big trading institutions. Simply put – Volume Profile can show you what will happen in the future!

Why Care about Volumes and What the Big Institutions Are Doing?

There is a straightforward reason why we need to know what the big financial institutions are doing. The reason is that they dominate, move, and manipulate the markets. It is they who decide where the price will go, not you or I. We are too small.

Take a look at following picture. It shows the 10 biggest banks and how much volume they control. Together it is almost 65% of the market. Just 10 banks!

It is those guys who own this game. Those are the guys we need to track and follow. And how do we follow them? By using Volume Profile to track their volumes.

Rank	Name	Market share
1	JP Morgan	9.81 %
2	Deutsche Bank	8.41 %
3	Citi	7.87 %
4	XTX Markets	7.22 %
5	UBS	6.63 %
6	State Street Corporation	5.50 %
7	HCTech	5.28 %
8	HSBC	4.93 %
9	Bank of America Merrill Lynch	4.63 %
10	Goldman Sachs	4.50 %

Volume Profile – Trading Setups

In this chapter, I will show you my most favorite Volume Profile setups. You can use these setups to identify strong Support and Resistance zones. When the price reaches these zones at some point in the future, you can use Order Flow to help you trade there!

What you will find the most helpful for this will be the Order Flow confirmation strategies. These will help you tell if the big market participants are active in those zones and if they are going to trade them. If the big guys start joining the party around a strong Volume Profile-based S/R zone, then it will be a strong confirmation signal for you. Such a signal indicates that the S/R is most likely going to work!

These Volume Profile setups can be used with any time frame. However, this book focuses on intraday trading, and for that, I suggest you use these setups with 30 Minute time frame. You can also go to 15 Minute or 1 Hour, but I would not advise going past that.

This is my favorite trading setup. It is based on the fact that big trading institutions first need to enter their huge trading positions before manipulating the market into a new trend. They enter their huge positions in a rotation. This is the only place where they can accumulate such large volume without being seen and without their intentions being recognised.

You can trade it in three steps:

1. Look for a price rotation/tight channel that is followed by a strong uptrend (or a downtrend). What happens in such a formation is that big institutions are accumulating their trading positions (in the rotation) and then they start the trend. A Long scenario looks like this:

2. Use Volume Profile in the rotation area to identify where the heaviest volumes were. The area where the heaviest volumes got traded is a strong Support (Long trade scenario).

3. When the price enters this Support zone in the future, open your Order Flow and wait for any of the confirmation setups to appear there. Jump in the trade as soon as it gets confirmed on the Order Flow.

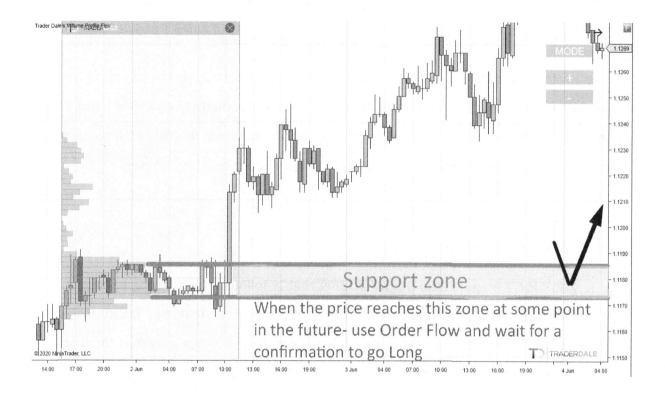

When the price reaches this zone at some point in the future- use Order Flow and wait for a confirmation to go Long

The Logic Behind Volume Accumulation Setup

Let me now explain the logic behind this setup. There are two reasons (factors) why the price reacts to these volume zones so nicely. This reasoning also applies to all the other volume setups I am going to show you later.

Reason #1: Strong Buyers/Sellers who were accumulating their positions are likely to defend their positions. As a result of this, when the price returns to the volume accumulation area, strong Buyers/Sellers actively defend their positions.

Strong Buyers start aggressively buying to drive the price upwards again to defend the level where they accumulated their Longs. Strong Sellers defend their Shorts positions by aggressive selling, which moves the price lower again. Here is a picture to demonstrate this (a Long trade scenario):

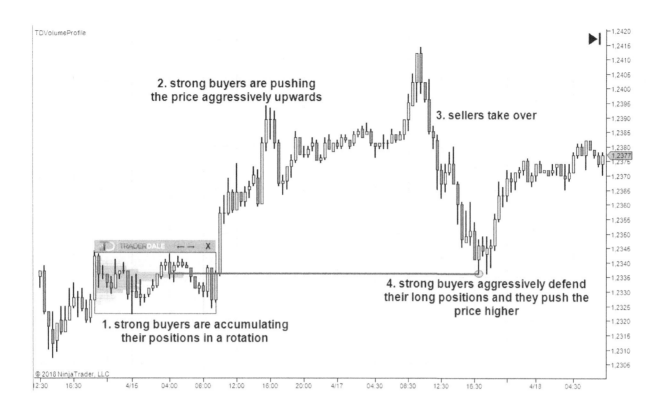

Reason #2: Nobody wants to risk a fight with strong and aggressive Buyers/Sellers.

Let me demonstrate this by using an example: First, strong Buyers accumulated their positions in a sideways rotation. Then they pushed the price aggressively upwards (this is the Long scenario of Setup #1). After that, the Buyers stopped pushing the price upwards for a while, and Sellers took over. They were pushing the price lower and lower, but when they approached the strong rotation where the aggressive Buyers had accumulated their massive positions, the Sellers stopped their selling activity and closed their positions. Why? Because they didn't want to risk a fight with strong and aggressive Buyers.

When somebody who is in a Short position wants to close their position, he buys. So, when those Sellers start to buy to get rid of their Short positions, they actually help to drive the price upwards.

Let me make this clearer with a picture:

It is the combination of these two factors that drives the price away from the Support/Resistance zones.

Example #1: Volume Accumulation Setup

Example #2: Volume Accumulation Setup

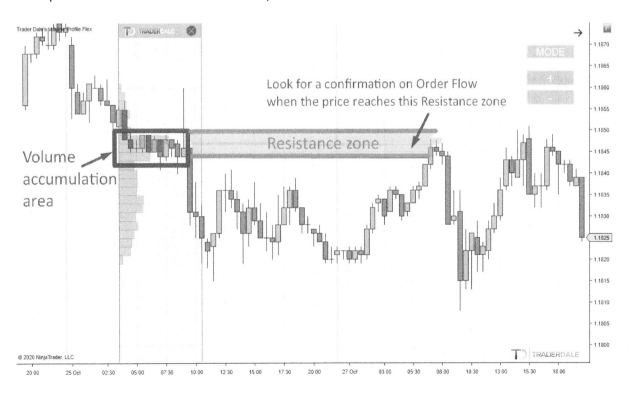

Example #3: Volume Accumulation Setup

Example #4: Volume Accumulation Setup

Volume Profile Setup #2: Trend Setup

This is also one of my favorite Volume Profile setups. It is based on the fact that there is not much time for accumulating big trading positions when there is a trend. Sometimes, the trend movement halts for a bit and some new and relatively big volumes get accumulated. Those volumes show as a little "bump" on the otherwise thin Volume Profile. Those "bumps" are called Volume Clusters. Those Volume Clusters often work as strong Support and Resistance zones when the price gets back to them in the future. Here are exact steps on how to trade this:

1. Trade this setup when there is a strong trend. If there is an uptrend, you will want to trade Longs. If it is a downtrend, then it is Shorts.

2. When you have found a trend (in this case an uptrend), use Volume Profile to see how the volume was distributed throughout the trend move.

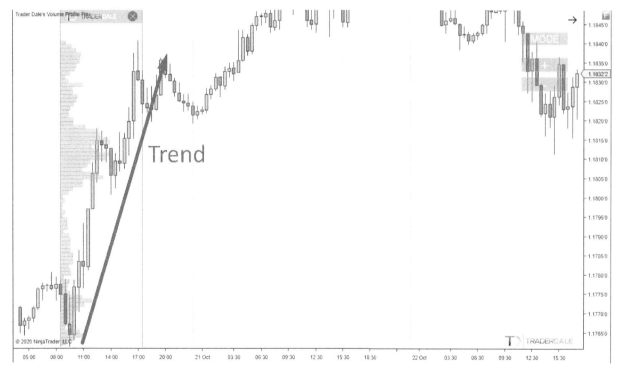

3. Look for significant Volume Clusters that were created within the trend. In the picture below, there is one significant Volume Cluster. The area where the volumes were the heaviest is a Support.

4. When the price enters this Support area, open your Order Flow and wait for any of the confirmation setups to appear there. You jump in the trade as soon as it gets confirmed on the OF.

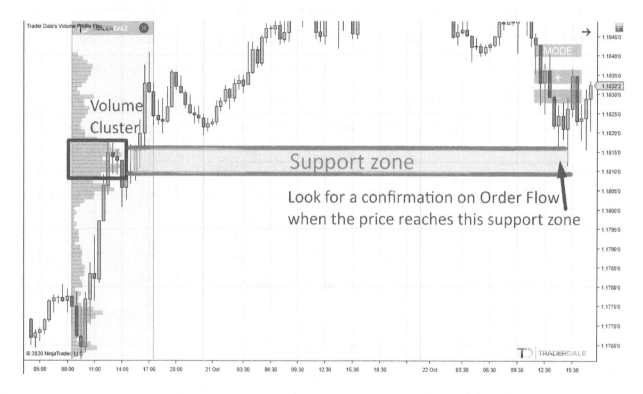

The Logic behind the Trend Setup:

The logic behind this setup is that Buyers were pushing the price upwards and they were adding to their Long positions in the place where we now see the Volume Cluster. When the price hits the Volume Cluster again, those Buyers are likely to become active again and begin to defend their Long positions they placed there earlier. This will push the price up from this Volume Cluster again.

The same two factors that help to move the price and which I mentioned with the Volume Accumulation setup apply here as well.

EXAMPLES: Trend Setup

Example #1: Trend Setup

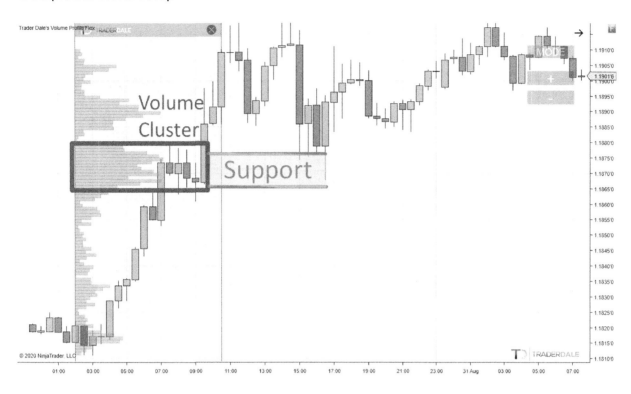

Example #2: Trend Setup

Example #3: Trend Setup

Example #4: Trend Setup

Volume Profile Setup #3: Rejection Setup

This setup is based on finding a very strong rejection of either higher or lower prices and applying Flexible Volume Profile to it in order to spot strong Volume Clusters.

The key to trading this setup successfully is in identifying the strong rejection in the chart. Sometimes, the strong rejection looks like a strong pin bar created at a swing point. However, sometimes it is not so clear and there is a different candle pattern. I don't care what pattern there is because usually the pattern changes with the time frame (and I don't like being bound by a time frame). What matters the most is that the rejection is strong and that the aggressiveness within it is evident.

In a Long trade scenario, I look for selling activity followed by a sudden price reversal and strong buying activity. For example, like this:

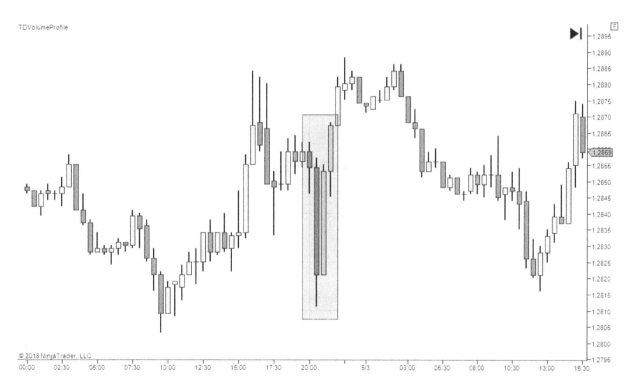

In a Short trade scenario, I look for buying activity followed by sudden price reversal and strong selling activity. For example, like this:

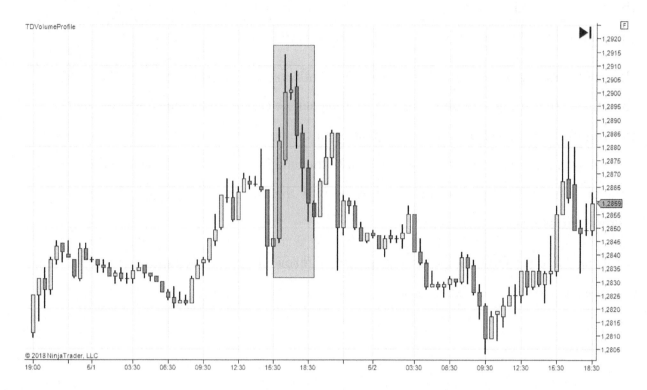

When there is a strong price reversal, we get the information that one side of the market became very aggressive and strongly rejected some price level. When this happens, I am interested in how the volumes were distributed within the rejection. In other words, I am interested in the place where the heaviest volumes within the rejection were added to the market. The reason for that is that the place with the heaviest volumes marks the place where the counterparty was the most aggressive—the place where the biggest fight was.

Here is how to trade this:

1. Use the Flexible Volume Profile to look into a strong rejection area to see where the volumes were the heaviest. There needs to be a nice and strong Volume Cluster there.

2. The area where the Volume Cluster got formed is a zone of S/R. Wait until the price comes back there again. When it does, open the Order Flow software to look for a trade confirmation.

3. If there is a rejection of higher prices, then you want to enter a Short position.

If there is a rejection of lower prices, then you want to enter a Long position. See the example below:

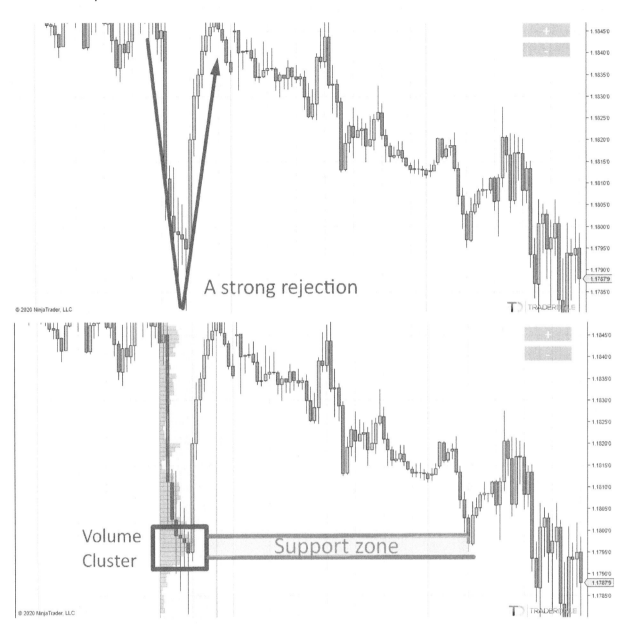

The Volume Profile Setup #3 is the most difficult setup to trade because sometimes it is hard to tell when the rejection was really strong and aggressive. Sometimes the rejection is pretty strong but the distribution of volumes within the rejection is not easy to read—mostly when there are stronger volume areas within the rejection itself. Because of this, it takes some time and practice to master this setup

EXAMPLES: Rejection Setup

Here are some more examples of the Rejection Setup.

Example #1: Rejection Setup

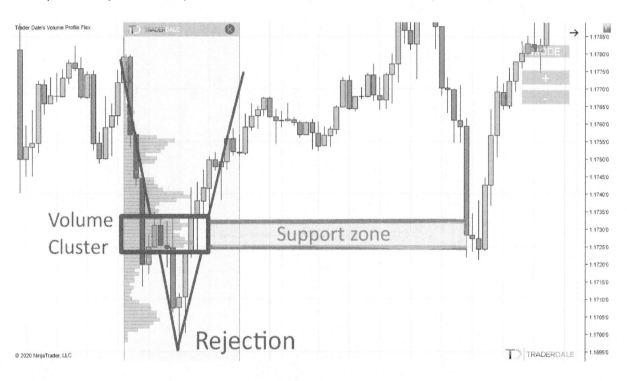

Example #2: Rejection Setup

Example #3: Rejection Setup

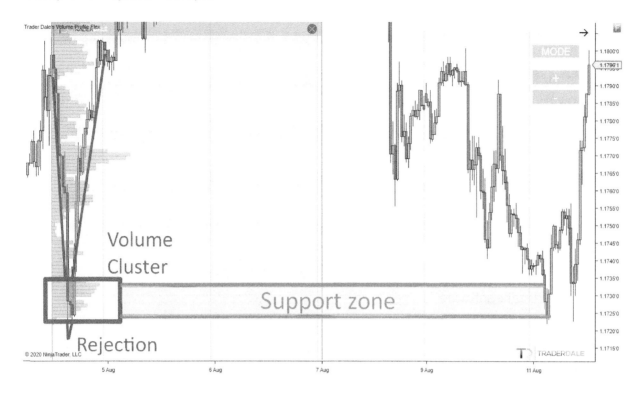

Example #4: Rejection Setup

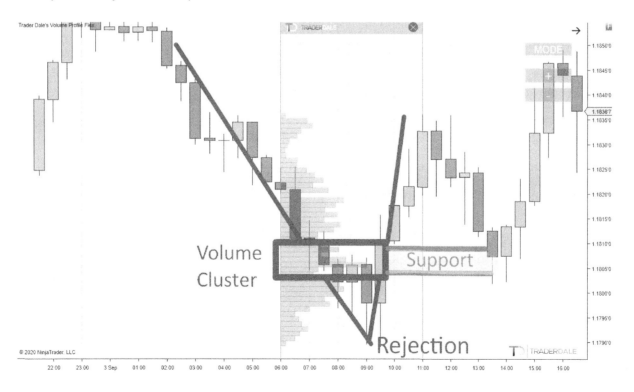

Where to Get More Info about Volume Profile

Volume Profile is a fantastic tool that definitely deserves more of your attention. As this book's main goal is to teach you Order Flow trading, I won't go more in depth with Volume Profile. However, you can learn more about it on my website www.trader-dale.com. What you will find there is a free copy of my book *VOLUME PROFILE: The Insider's Guide to Trading* available for you to download.

If you would like to go even deeper, I suggest you get my **Order Flow Pack** (available here: https://www.trader-dale.com/order-flow-indicator-and-video-course/). This pack includes:

- Order Flow software
- Volume Profile software
- Extensive Order Flow and Volume Profile video training

If you would just like to get the Volume Profile software, you can get it on my website here: (https://www.trader-dale.com/volume-profile-forex-trading-course/)

Live Trading Examples - Link

I first planned to comment on some of my Order Flow + Volume Profile live trades here, but the written format makes it quite difficult and not so effective. For this reason, I set up a special webpage for you where I uploaded a couple of live trading videos. You can see me trading with Order Flow and Volume Profile in those videos using all the tips and approaches I showed you in this book. Here is the link:

Link: https://www.trader-dale.com/of-book/

Password: happy trading

What to Do Next

In this book, I tried my best to explain my trading strategies and give you a good starting point for using them independently. I hope you liked it and that you find the way of trading alongside the big trading institutions using Order Flow and Volume Profile as appealing as I do. This book should give you the basics you need to start exploring more and, most importantly, get some firsthand experience.

Trading using the Order Flow is like driving a car. All the theory about driving is one thing, but actually driving a car is an experience you won't be able to learn from a book. You actually need to sit in the car and drive. This is what will make you a good driver, not reading books about driving.

The actual process of driving (or trading) will also become way more natural when you start doing it. I expect that after going through this Order Flow book, your head could feel a bit dizzy from the amount of information, especially if Order Flow is entirely new for you. There are just so many things to watch, so many nuances, so many things to remember, right? Well, theoretically, yes. BUT when you start using Order Flow in your trading, many of these things will become natural for you. In a short amount of time, reading the Order Flow will become way easier, and when you look at it, you will see a clear picture, not just a sum of cells, numbers, and different shades of colors.

What you need now is to practice the things you have learned. You need practice and hands-on experience!

Accelerate Your Learning!

To accelerate your learning and give you as much information as possible, I have created a number of special training courses. There are two in particular that I highly recommend getting. They are called The Elite Pack and The Order Flow Pack. Each one of them focuses on different things. Let me now tell you what those two training packs consist of and how they can help you!

The Elite Pack

The Elite Pack is ideal for you if you would like to perfect your trading with Volume Profile. This Pack focuses on intraday, swing trading, and long-term investment trading with Price Action, Volume Profile, and VWAP.

It consists of four main parts:

1. **Volume Profile Video Course:** a 15-hour-long video course on trading with Volume Profile, Price Action, and VWAP. It consists of an in-depth explanation of my favorite and proven trading strategies and includes hundreds of real trading examples.

2. **Dale's Trading Levels:** After you have gone through the whole video course, I suggest you start following me in my everyday trading. Each day I will give you my personal intraday and swing trading levels, which are based on the strategies you learned. I explain all my trading levels in a daily video, which you will get every day as well. This way, you will know what and how I am going to trade that day and the reasoning behind my decisions.

   I think the best way to learn something is to follow somebody who has a lot of experience. This is a very effective, proven, and fast way to learn!

3. **Volume Profile + VWAP Indicators:** The Elite Pack includes a lifetime license to my custom-made Volume Profile and VWAP indicators. Those indicators were developed by expert developers precisely to my needs. They are fast, precise, reliable, and versatile (you can use them for all trading instruments) and they have all the functions you will need for successful trading.

4. **Community & Support:** Apart from all this, you will also get access to my trading community and trading forum, where you can discuss your trading with other members. It goes without saying that you will also get my personal unlimited email support. Whatever you need to help with, shoot me an email and I will do my best to help.

BONUS: As a special bonus to all of this, our specially trained tech support will do the complete setup for you! They will install the trading platform with all my indicators, create workspaces (exactly the same as I use), and connect you to a reliable data feed—for FREE. This way, you will be able to start learning immediately, without any delays!

The Elite Pack

Dale's recommended educational pack includes:

Volume Profile Video Course

- 44 In-Depth Videos with 15+ Hours of training
- Complete NinjaTrader 8 Setup Guide
- Learn the most profitable setups I use each day
- Hundreds of REAL trade examples to help you learn to trade ASAP
- Works on all trading instruments (Forex, Futures, Stocks, etc)

Dale's Trading Levels

- Daily Trading Levels / Signals & Video
- Monthly Swing Levels / Signals and Video
- Video Guide to Trading Dale's Daily Levels
- Access to the Member Forum
- Full email support

Volume Profile Pack

- Multiple Computers / Lifetime Access
- Flexible Volume Profile (NinjaTrader 8)
- Fixed Volume Profile (NinjaTrader 8)
- Flexible Volume Profile (MT4)
- Install & Quick Start Guide for each Indicator

The Elite Pack is available at: www.trader-dale.com

The Order Flow Pack

The Order Flow pack is ideal for you if you would like to perfect your Order Flow trading. If you finished this book and liked what you learned here, I would definitely recommend continuing your learning with the Order Flow Pack.

The Order Flow pack consists of four main parts:

1. **Order Flow Video Course:** A 12-hour long in-depth video course where I teach you all you need to know to trade with Order Flow successfully. It covers Order Flow trading strategies, entry and exit strategies, confirmation strategies, live trading, Order Flow settings ... simply put, all that you need to feel confident trading with the Order Flow! The video course is a very practical and right-to-the-point guide. No fluff, just all the useful info, put in a logical order, and all in one place.

2. **Order Flow and Delta Software:** My custom-made software, which I developed for my own intraday trading. It is a versatile tool that you can use for all trading instruments (Forex included) and has many very useful and unique features and other OF software lacks. This software is constantly updated and new features are being added.

3. **Volume Profile Software:** Order Flow combined with Volume Profile is a very powerful combo. Use my custom-made Volume Profile indicator to see the big picture and to identify strong institutional Support and Resistance zones. Then use Order Flow to confirm your trade entry, pinpoint the best place to enter your trade, and manage your trade like a professional, institutional trader!

4. **Lifetime Support:** Getting the Order Flow pack will get you also my unlimited email support. Have questions regarding setups, settings, trades, or have you run into some technical difficulties? I am here to help!

BONUS: Our specially trained tech support will do the complete Order Flow and Volume Profile setup for you! They will install the trading platform with all my indicators, create workspaces (exactly the same as I use), and connect you to a reliable data feed. No need to read manuals; just jump right into learning and trading!

Order Flow Pack

This day-trading pack includes:

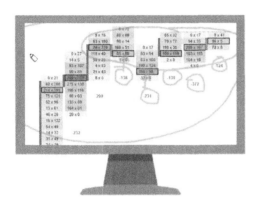

Order Flow Video Course

- 39 In-depth videos with 12+ hours of training
- Learn the most profitable OF setups I use each day
- Learn how to use OF to confirm your trade entries
- Learn how to use OF to manage your trades
- Advanced Volume Profile training
- Complete NinjaTrader 8 Setup Guide

Order Flow Software

- My custom-made Order Flow software
- Fast, precise, reliable
- Many unique features to help you read the market
- Works with all trading instruments, including Forex
- Constantly updated

Volume Profile Pack

- Multiple Computers / Lifetime Access
- Flexible Volume Profile (NinjaTrader 8)
- Fixed Volume Profile (NinjaTrader 8)
- Flexible Volume Profile (MT4)
- Install & Quick Start Guide for each Indicator

The Order Flow Pack is available at: www.trader-dale.com

Just a Few Testimonials on My Trading Courses

Excellent Content and Service

After consuming hours of free content (all great I must add) I decided to buy the VP indicator for MT4 and Dale's online book. A great buy, but I soon realized I wanted to know more about Order Flow and all the bits and bobs. Dale had a fresh approach and I was eager to learn more.

Before I purchased the Elite Pack I asked many questions. Dale and his team answered every single one in a timely manner and with a personal touch. I felt right at home. From our first interaction the support has been unbelievable and the course content incredibly informative. I have learnt more in the past month than the last 36. The only thing I regret is not finding him three years ago.

Dale is a straight shooter. Not promising you the Holy Grail of trading and will point out successes and failures. It is refreshing!

Great Course, Great Indicators and Damn Good Value

There are many trading gurus to choose from. The challenge is finding one that is good, honest and knows what he is talking about. Trader Dale is one of those. He focuses on volume-based trading methods rather than the traditional price and time methods. It is a different and very interesting approach and one that has great potential for me. I have studied several different trading styles and used several different markets. So far, none have worked as expected and this is because they were all missing something. That something is volume. Trader Dale clearly explains why volume is so important and how to use it. His teaching methods are clear and concise and he explains everything you need to know. His indicators for MT4 and NT8 are top class. The price he charges for his training and indicators is very reasonable. I have no hesitation in recommending him to anyone who really wants to understand the market better and to get the edge that will propel you forwards. This is not a get-rich-quick scheme. There is a lot to learn and understand, but Trader Dale does a fantastic job of explaining everything. He gives you the theory and then shows real examples of how it works. He shows winners as well as losses and uses different markets to prove that it works. Take the plunge and get the professional training and support you deserve—you will not regret it.

Invaluable, very insightful and clear training

I couldn't trade without Trader Dale's Flexible Volume Profile or Order Flow. His explanations and training seem to cover every aspect of the volume profile or order flow and are very clear to understand. I was shocked when he explained something in his Order Flow training. For years I've wanted to understand Order Flow and I watched hours of video and attended countless webinars from individuals claiming they were going to teach how it works and no one ever mentioned one simple point about something that shows up frequently in Order Flow throughout the day. Dale was only one who pointed it out and explained it very clearly and, for me, it made Order Flow immediately usable. I've never gotten the feeling he was holding something back for a future purchase, I do believe he shares all he knows and sincerely wants to see others succeed. Very rare.

Reliable and helpful person, professional and excellent services!

I found Dale's wonderful book *Volume Profile - The Insider's Guide to Trading* by chance. Only reading the beginning of his book I knew that was what I was looking for. Then the book led me to his website and training courses. He surprised me with his extreme helpfulness and kindness. Whenever I am confused, he's willing to help with all of his kindness and more than I expect. I've never met anyone who is kind-hearted and helpful like him. Moreover, not only his invented Volume Profile indicator but his professional trading methods absolutely impress me. I do not know what words to say, but I would like to say: Thank God I found him as my tutor/ trainer/ advisor in trading. If you are interested in trading and would like to develop your trading, please join him and you will never be disappointed.

Quality individual that gives excellent training and market guidance

I discovered Trader Dale's service a little over six months ago and have been absolutely thrilled with the knowledge he has shared in that time. Because of the incredible market insights he shares with his members, along with the extensive training materials he provides, I have become a much improved trader.

And the best part is I can now trade with confidence and not with fear. Because of Trader Dale's training and market analysis, which includes expected outcomes at well-defined Volume Profile levels, I can trade with total confidence.

Yes, there are losses, but because of the "risk-controlled" training plan he has shared, the losses are minimal and rare compared to the successful trades and profits.

I am so happy I found this service.

Trader Dale—the most honest and reliable Trading School

Based on my personal experience with the link trading market, I found the most reliable, honest and simple trading ideas are located under Trader Dale webpages. Really it can be considered a Trading School especially for beginners. It can convert beginners to profitable traders in a short period. My experience started early but within three months studying Trader Dale courses – VP, OF & VWAP – I converted my trial from Demo version to profitable live trading, which I am happy with now. I need to express my thanks to Mr. Dale for his efforts and keen support of his site members. Really I highly recommend beginners to depend on Trader Dale's website.

Unique Style of Trading with Full Dedication in Teaching

Dale is a real trader who loves to trade and help people make a decent living out of trading. I have been struggling to trade with a number of systems available in the market. I went to different gurus even but could not discipline myself and my trading sucked big time.

After learning from Dale about the Volume Profile, my trading results changed dramatically and I could literally stop over trading and count my profits. Though my progress is slow 'cause I already lost a lot of money and my capital is smaller in comparison to other traders, the gem I know from Dale now can definitely help me to build a fortune sooner or later. I believe that.

Significantly, the daily levels are really helpful for busy people like me, which makes trading easier and faster.

Thanks, Dale, for your wonderful support. I don't usually rate mentors in any review website, but if my review counts and supports your program in any way, that is my small gesture of showing gratitude for your hard work teaching me how to profit well.

Excellent

There is not hype with this guy, none. It is very easy to understand, for me I have been trading and researching now for about two years and I already used the Volume Profile, but this guy just explained everything about TA and institutions and how they trade and the things that go on behind the scenes that I assumed were the way he explains them, so this guy has basically confirmed every suspicion I have had on how the market really moves and why. A lot of people since I have been learning TA go off the deep end with it, and they literally start treating and thinking of the market like it will run all by itself without any people playing and it's just one big machine running on its own, or why 90% of all the TA bulls*** out there doesn't work and the questions I have asked while learning this stuff and why so much didn't really fit. Anyways, if anyone is at the point I am with not wanting to work for a firm, but deeply desiring to learn how and why the markets really move, then follow this guy. And the plus side is when you fully understand that you literally have to follow big money and stop thinking you're going to really do something out there, you'll also be amazed at just how easy trading really is. Thanks again, Dale, I have been waiting to find someone like you for about two years now.

Glossary

Ask: Is displayed on the right side of the footprint. It shows how many contracts were traded there with Market Buy order and also with Limit Sell order.

Bid: Is displayed on the left side of the footprint. It shows how many contracts were traded there with Market Sell order and also with Limit Buy order.

Cumulative Delta: Sum of all Deltas of the current day. Its calculation starts every day anew.

Delta: A difference between Bid and Ask. It is calculated as: Ask – Bid. Positive Delta indicates strong buyers and negative Delta indicates strong sellers.

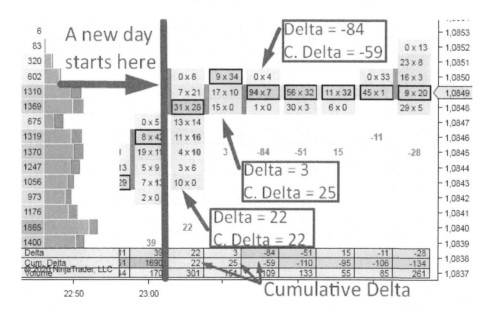

Footprint: A box that represents a standard price "candle" with the Bid and Ask values displayed.

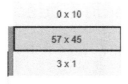

High Volume Node (HVN): A black outline in every footprint pointing to the price where the heaviest volumes got traded (within that footprint).

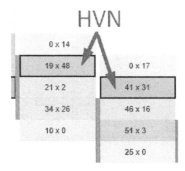

Iceberg Order: When a big trading institution enters a position, they sometimes don't enter it all at once with one order. Instead, their algorithms split the order into many small orders. For example, instead of entering 10 contracts, they enter 1+1+1... They do this super quick.

Imbalance: If Ask is 300% or more than Bid, then it is a Buying Imbalance = Buyers are way stronger than Sellers. If Bid is 300% or more than Ask, then it is a Selling Imbalance = Sellers are way stronger than Buyers. Imbalances are marked in blue. Note that Bid and Ask are compared diagonally from left to right!

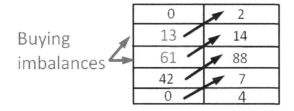

Multiple Node: Two or more High Volume Nodes next to each other. My software highlights them in yellow. Multiple Nodes represent Support/Resistance zones.

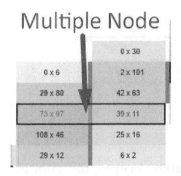

Stacked Imbalance: Three or more Buying or Selling Imbalances on top of each other.

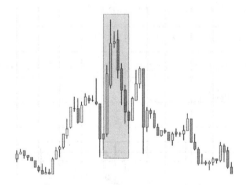

Strong Rejection: Price goes aggressively one way and then suddenly reverses and goes aggressively the other way.

Support/Resistance: A price level or zone in the chart where we expect that the price will react to (bounce off) it.

Risk Reward Ratio (RRR): Potential gain versus the potential loss of a trade. If you use Stop Loss = 10 pips and Take Profit = 10 pips, then RRR = 1. If you use SL = 10 pips and TP = 20 pips, then RRR = 2.

Unfinished Business: A market imperfection. When the market went one way then turned the other way without having the high/low formed properly. A properly formed high needs to have 0 contracts traded at the Bid, and a properly formed Low needs to have 0 contracts traded at the Ask.

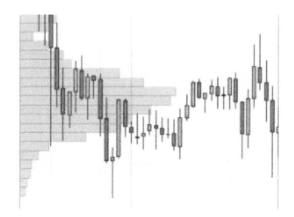

Volume Accumulation: An area (usually a price rotation area) where heavy volumes were traded.

Volume Cluster: Area in a chart where heavy volumes were traded. Often appears in a trend or in a Rejection.

Thank you!

At this place, I would like to thank you for reading my book. I hope you liked it, and that you found it useful. I wish it helps you in achieving your financial goals and dreams no matter how big they are!

Happy trading!

-Dale

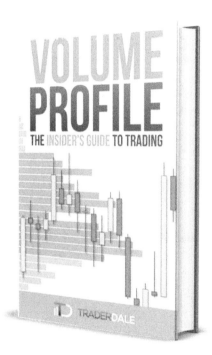

VOLUME PROFILE:
The Insider's Guide To Trading

What will you learn:

- How to work with Price Action
- Price Action strategies that you can immediately put to use
- How Volume Profile works
- My favorite Volume Profile strategies
- How to find your own trading style and what are the best trading instruments to trade
- How to manage trading around macroeconomic news
- How to do your market analysis from A to Z
- How to manage your positions
- How to do a proper money management
- How to deal with trading psychology
- How to do a proper backtest and how to get started with trading your backtested strategies
- What are the most common trading mistakes and how to avoid them
- The exact ways and rules I apply to my own trading

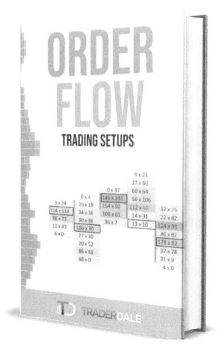

ORDER FLOW: Trading Setups

What will you learn:

- Choosing the right trading platform for Order Flow trading
- NinjaTrader 8 platform – introduction
- Choosing the right Order Flow software
- Where to get data for Order Flow
- The best instruments to trade with Order Flow
- Order Flow – what it tells us
- Order Flow – special features
- How to set up Order Flow workspace
- Order Flow – trading setups
- Order Flow – confirmation setups
- How to use Order Flow to determine your Take Profit and Stop Loss
- How to use Order Flow for trade management
- How to find strong institutional Supports and Resistances using Volume Profile
- How to combine Order Flow with Volume Profile

Made in the USA
Las Vegas, NV
12 January 2024

84253340R00090